ON THE WINGS OF PHOENIX RISING

A JOURNEY FROM ASHES TO JOY

Yuan Miao

Translated by Denis Mair and Peter Shiao

Copyright © 2013 by Yuan Miao

All rights reserved. No part of this publication may be reproduced, distributed, or transmitted in any form or by any means, including photocopying, recording, or other electronic or mechanical methods, without the prior written permission of the publisher, except in the case of brief quotations embodied in critical reviews and certain other noncommercial uses permitted by copyright law. For permission requests, write to the publisher at the address below.

Phoenix Century Press
P.O. Box 1792
Sausalito, CA 94966

www.phoenixcenturypress.com

Printed in the United States of America

The author of this book does not dispense medical advice or prescribe the use of any technique as a form of treatment for physical, emotional, or medical problems without the advice of a physician, either directly or indirectly. The intent of the author is only to offer information of a general nature to help readers in their quest for emotional and spiritual well-being. In the event they use any of the information in this book for themselves, which is their constitutional right, the author and the publisher assume no responsibility for their actions.

On the Wings of Phoenix Rising:
A Journey from Ashes to Joy

by Yuan Miao

Translated by Denis Mair and Peter Shiao

Introduction by Judith Simon Prager, Ph.D.

Cover and interior design by Gary Newman
www.newmango.com

ISBN-10: 0989731618
ISBN-13: 978-0-9897316-1-4

For further information:
www.ncfinternational.org
www.yuanmiaolaolao.com

Portions of this book were previously published as part of *Dancing on Rooftops with Dragons*. This book includes a new preface by Yuan Miao written for this edition, as well as the following new material: "Return to True Nature," "Baja Elements" and "A Story about Hair."

Table of Contents

Introduction 1
Preface 4
How I Came to Write This Book 7
PART I: IN THE WORLD OF SAMSARA 13
   1. My Grandmother and I 15
   2. Leaving Home at Age Three 20
   3. Fear of Death at Age Seven 24
   4. Taking a Life at Age Ten 28
   5. My First Love 31
   6. My Uncle 35
   7. Peony in Springtime 40
   8. Seventh Month of the Year 1985 46
   9. An Unintentional Vow 51
  10. Those "Poor Monks"...Why Are They So Poor? 56
  11. Grandma Goes Home 61
  12. Even My Daughter Is Gone 65
  13. Suicidal Encounters 70
  14. Uniting with the Way of Heaven:
      Taking All Faiths as My Teachers 77
  15. Travelers in the Bardo Realm 82

16. A Glorious Procession of Rinpoches 92
17. Leave Everything and Go to America! 101
18. I Shall Guide and Protect You 105
19. Who Is the Shining One? 110
20. Universal Masters 118
21. How to Receive Guidance from Heavenly Masters 136
22. A Great Prophecy 147
23. Who Am I in the Infinite Game? 153

PART II: PHOENIX RISING 159
24. About Yoga of Joy 161
25. Return to True Nature 175
26. Baja Elements 185
27. A Story about Hair 190

Introduction

The telling question is:
Are you related to the infinite?

— Carl Jung

How can we answer Carl Jung's question? Truly, who and what are we if we are *not* related to the infinite? And yet, as we stand with our feet on the earth, from what perch, from what vantage point, can we see our way to touching the eternal? The poet Robert Browning said, "Ah, but a man's reach must exceed his grasp, or what's a heaven for?" But what if instead of reaching, heaven comes to *you,* and invites you to dance?

If you are Yuan Miao, invited to bring wisdom to the world, you join the dance only at your peril. Because the path is not strewn with flowers and accolades, but with sacrifice and suffering. The price is very high, and yet, irresistibly, the value is immeasurable.

So often we look to mystical people to explain the universe and all creation to us. Like children, like supplicants, we come before them saying, "Why is it that *such-and-such* happened?" and "Why can't things be *this* way instead of that?"

And if we are more evolved, we ask, *"How is it, really?"* and, even, *"How is it that you know?"*

When Yuan Maio was an innocent child of three, her father—angry at her grandmother but unable to act it out—raised his heavy Korean War surplus boots and kicked his tiny daughter across the room. It was then that her journey began. That kick sent Yuan Maio out of body and into the arms of Guanyin, the Chinese Buddhist deity of compassion and mercy, who told her, "When you are grown, come back with an empty vase, and I will teach you." This is the story of how it is, really, and how it is that Yuan Maio knows.

Yuan Maio grew up in Communist China with Buddhist grandparents who were disgraced and destroyed for their beliefs. Somehow, she flourished in that place, becoming a famous producer of documentaries for the largest Chinese TV network. She had a handsome husband, a beautiful daughter, fame, success.

But Guanyin awaited her mystical awakening. And like something out of *Crouching Tiger, Hidden Dragon*, the awakening exploded before her eyes and imploded within her body. And the mystical path proved steep and costly.

Maybe as you read this story you will have the sensations I had: wishing to be anointed by the spirit world into the secrets of the ancients. And then, when the vow of suffering is taken, gasping as Yuan Miao loses everything—even more than the fame and fortune she thought she had agreed to sacrifice.

It is very complex and dangerous to dance with the forces of other planes. Seductive and overwhelming. And we watch and wonder about the depth of our own courage, as all that Yuan Miao holds dear disappears before her eyes.

If that were the end of her story, this would be a tragedy, but Guanyin had not deserted her, and Yuan Miao's life took yet another turn, flooding her with the wisdom and the joyful practice that she passes on to all those who pick up this book.

Oh reader, come with an empty vase and read this book for two important reasons. One is that you will never forget the story of this beautiful Chinese woman who had it all, lost it all, and found her true self in ways both surprisingly mystical and breath-takingly true. The second reason is more urgent: it is that just reading about *her* journey could forever change *yours*.

—*Judith Simon Prager*

Judith Simon Prager, Ph.D., author of *Journey to Alternity: Transformational Healing Through Stories and Metaphors* and *The Worst Is Over: What To Say When Every Moment Counts.*

Preface

There are three strings of numbers that have mattered a great deal in my life. One is 7/15/1985, the day when large globes of light descended from the sky onto the roof of my house, rousing me from dreams of a common mortal life. The second is 11/11/1999, when a midnight revelation told me to "put down my involvements and travel to America," where I have done my part to pave the way towards a zenith of human civilization to be created from a fusion of Western and Eastern wisdom traditions, under the aegis of a new celestial dispensation. The third number, 2050, came to me as a revelation from a timeless cosmic source, as the year for phoenix-rebirth in this new century.

Aside from glimpses into destiny offered by these numbers, the greatest revelation given me in this life was my Big-Footed Grandma. She midwifed my birth; she gave me my name; in my all-absorbing heart she planted seeds of wisdom. Her compassionate wisdom was the lamp that led me out of perplexity. Thus for me "Grandma" was not just a wise Tibetan woman, for she represented the maternal source of cosmic space-time. "Big-Footed" did not just apply to her shoe size, for it alluded to the "Path" she followed and her identity as a "wayfarer."

In my life's path I began by running away from home at age three and meeting a kind lady who looked down from mid-air. At age seven I had to overcome extreme fear over seeing a dead body. When I was eleven or twelve years of age, due to some perceived injustice I was suffering, I knelt on the ground and wept. I cannot recall the exact occasion, but I remember my heart being filled with a highly "mature" sense of resignation and despair. Suddenly I heard an old woman's voice, seeming to come from within my heart but also from outside: "That little girl who is crying is not your real self: you have a bigger self." I could not figure out the meaning but the voice reassured me considerably.

Then as a young mother I endured the illness and death of my only daughter, which brought me to the edge of suicide and finally led to my awakening. This book tells the story of what I went through in my topsy-turvy, tear-soaked course of growth, along the edge between life and death, as I became that "bigger self." It was a process much like a phoenix being reborn from fire.

Western readers may be interested to learn some key points from a dakini lineage of Himalayan emptiness-wisdom, which transmits realization about the underlying reality of birth-death cycles. Only on such a foundation can a person's life be filled with joy. In some sections of the book I speak of the "Yoga of Joy" in general, but the most detailed explanation focuses on the Ninth Step, which is "Return to True Nature." Because many modern people overly emphasize logical investigation at the expense of body-mind-spirit direct experience, I think that "Return to True Nature" can be quite helpful.

Also, as you read, please don't think you are simply reading just another person's story. I believe that if you read between the lines of each chapter and in the spaces between the words, there is something to find, a teaching to be discovered. Read in this deeper way, the material and energy of the story will forge for you, too, a deep connection to the ancestors and lineage, and may even transport you all the way back, to the maternal source of the universe.

I do not meet scholarly requirements and I do not indulge in elaborate logical reasoning. In dakini transmission it is forgivable to let go of these things.

I wish that each of you will be blessed to awaken from your suffering. May each of you keep your innocent thinking; may your mind remain empty and receptive; may your body remain full of innate intelligence. Like a phoenix reborn from flames, may you manifest the robust life force of your cosmic origins.

I would like to thank Diana Wong for her kind support and friendship, the Chinese gentleman Mr. Du Yong Qiang for his support of the New Century Foundation's mission, the Blue Pearl Group for showing that this teaching could be appreciated and practiced by Westerners, Denis Mair for his skill and artistry in translating these words from the original Chinese, Gary Newman for his time and expertise in the design of this book, and the many others who helped in myriad ways to make this book possible.

—Yuan Miao
California
June 14, 2013

How I Came to Write This Book

After quieting my mind of all external concerns, letting all return to silence, I face myself again.

When I worked as a documentary director for China Central Television, part of my work was to write scripts and background material for our projects. Back in 1987, I had spent three months writing a full-length novel in Chinese entitled *Light of Buddha*. I was moved to write it because that was an eventful period for me (including a visitation by light globes, as told in Chapter 8). However, this work was not a model of frankness. Given barriers to expression in the area of spirituality at that time, it would have been unrealistic to attempt anything more real and personal. More importantly, I had many doubts myself, and was deluded on several important points about the path of enlightenment. Thus the *Light of Buddha* went to print in a crude and shallow form.

Fortunately, sixteen years of experience as a filmmaker have tempered me to some degree. The aesthetic standard for documentary films is realism and simplicity. The production of documentary films had the effect of heightening my sensibility and critical perception of things. There are reasons why I have always loved this medium of communication. As a worldly training ground, Central Broadcasting exposed me to a little bit of everything—the noise and bustle of a television studio, the abundance of possibilities, the passing enthusiasms, the parading of celebrities and power-holders. In spite of it all I have always characterized my personal style as one stripped of all fancy wrappings, revealing only the essence.

Because of my spiritual experiences, every time I did a work-related writing project, a wish would always emerge: "When will I be able to write from where I live, not out of professional necessity, but as a natural expression of my life?"

In 1999 I resigned from my job and came to America. In a state of detachment from all worldly ties, my long-suppressed nature was soon manifested. While I was beset by visitors in a small room in San Gabriel, I casually scribbled several pages to show a few friends. The response was favorable, and people wanted to read more of what I had to say.

At that time, I had only been in America for six months. During those brief months, I had been in homes both luxurious and modest, and had seen patches of green among the chaparral-covered hills. What I mainly saw was the quiet desperation of Chinese people making their living in America. One day, looking through a car window, I told my friend at the wheel that someday soon I would move to a home in the mountains. Such a quiet setting would be ideal for my self-cultivation. My friend is a divorced mother of three who toils every day just to make ends meet. She laughed at my remark—clearly she gave no credence to my words. Later, I made the same prediction to another friend. This temperamental young friend couldn't help barking: "I have lived in America for eight years, but have only seen the mountains from the freeway. I know it would be nice to live in the mountains, but I never dared to believe I could. But I understand you. You have just arrived here, so it's natural to have fantasies about this place."

A fortunate opportunity let me meet a new friend, and a friend of hers—an artist. She showed me a book of this painter's work, and from the pages I sensed a familiar presence. I agreed to meet this painter and became acquainted the next day with Diana Wong—who had studied art in Italy. Her studio was by the ocean, but she also had a home in the mountains above Malibu beach—this was her place for silent retreats. Later she took me on a ride to look at her mountain retreat. As we were preparing to go back down the mountain, I gathered up my courage, and asked to stay alone in the mountains for a few days. After hesitating for a moment, she agreed.

Once alone, I began musing to myself. Knowing that this was the place answering to my presentiments where I could write my book, I did not have the audacity to make such an inordinate request of this newly met friend. Well then, better to dispense with illusory thinking, and simply follow the natural course of things. I would simply follow the path that the Compassionate Guanyin[1] was laying for me.

On the third day, as I gazed at a mother deer leading her two fawns just outside my window, and watched a red-bellied bird circling in the sky, the phone rang. It was Diana. She had had a peculiar dream, and wanted to tell me about it. She had dreamt of helping a

---

[1] Guanyin is the Chinese goddess of mercy and compassion, the Bodhisattva Avalokitesvara. A detailed description of her attributes and experiential manifestations are found starting on page 125.

girl dressed in red. This girl's mouth had been taped shut, and Diana used her hands to tear the seals so the girl could speak. She asked me whether I knew anything about this dream. "It appears that we should have a conversation," I responded, and proceeded to tell her that I had been thinking of writing a book that would reveal the secrets of my experiences. This would be a book to help people recognize the Truth, to turn away from suffering and find joy. Being a person of wisdom, Diana understood me right away. She volunteered to strip the seals that had been binding my mouth. She told me that if I was not afraid to live in the mountains by myself, I could stay there to write the book. My eyes were filled with tears at that very moment. The Compassionate Guanyin had used her all-embracing divine energy to arrange everything. I have gotten to know many well-meaning advisors, who have gravitated to me without my realizing it. Diana has become my friend on the path, and she is progressing rapidly while creating artworks from a place of meditative calm.

Under Diana's care and support, in October of 2000, I moved to Malibu to begin working on this book, and in March of the following year, *Joyful Yoga* (its original Chinese title), was finally in the hands of readers.

I have never experienced a writing process like this—it was nothing like a dramatic script or article. I found my own human faculties and logic becoming inconsequential during the writing process. There were times that I wanted to recall some aspects of my personal life—from family, parents, to my husband—that would perhaps make this work more readable, or valuable, or more sentimental. However, every time that I sat to write such chapters, I would experience a mental void, as if amnesia had set in and my past had been washed away. Memories of personal chapters of my life were certainly with me, but when trying to write them down, I would only experience a freeze. Even now there is no good explanation for this. Yet when I wrote about life in its essence, expressing realizations about the birth-death cycle, the writing process became extremely smooth, as if it were being empowered and guided. Then my heavenly master told me I had entered a state of mantric writing. This may explain why some readers say they feel a pure energy associated with the words, and they are guided to finish the book at one sitting.

I remember picking up my pen to write the title of the first chapter—*"My Grandmother and I."* From the moment I wrote those words I cried and wrote, wrote and cried. I never thought that the truthful manifestation of life would be like this. What was more, I did not expect that deep within my soul such stubborn attachment to self would remain. I even secretly wished that I would leave this earth upon finishing the book, making it my final testament. Exposing the vicissitudes of my life for all to see was something I was certainly not accustomed to. I knew that in writing this book, I was presenting to the world my own treasured experiences, which up to then had been just for me. I was also opening myself to others' doubts, laughter and judgment. As the writing and tears continued, I renounced my remaining attachments to personal privacy and wishes for undisturbed quietude.

Now, upon entering complete silence, I look at the surrounding mountains and ask myself whether there are more things I must discard? No, no.

In closing, I would like to remind the reader that this book does not follow the format of an autobiography. It is more like a documentary film that does not follow a strict chronology of events.

Here, I wish to praise all the high masters, teachers, and wise, good-hearted friends whose blessings and help have enabled me to tell this story like a child, without reservation or hindrance.

—Yuan Miao

OM MANE PADME HUM!

PART I

IN THE WORLD OF SAMSARA

— 1 —

My Grandmother and I

There are many stories about my grandmother's background, some of which verge on the fantastic. That she had big feet, however, is a well-known fact. My maternal great grandfather, surnamed Gao, came from a long lineage of wealth. His family had large land and business holdings in a suburb about seventy kilometers outside of Beijing, in a place called Zhuozhou. Because of this, the locals called him "Thousand-Hectare Gao."

By the time my grandfather became head of the household, however, the Gao family was already in financial decline, because Thousand-Hectare Gao had donated much of his wealth toward the building of various Buddhist temples, from the famed White Stupa outside the Forbidden City to the Sleeping Buddha Temple in the suburbs of Beijing. I have also heard that he generously sponsored "porridge offerings" on the first and fifteenth of each lunar month[2] in

---

2 The full moon falls on the fifteenth day of each lunar month, and the new moon comes on the first. These are important days to Buddhists for holding prayers, initiations and ceremonies.

the Dazhalan district of Beijing. A "porridge offering" entails cooking large amounts of rice porridge, then feeding it to the poor. This was toward the end of the Qing Dynasty period in China (early 1900's).

In my grandmother's era, it was still fashionable for females in the interior of China to bind their feet—this represented a good upbringing, and a woman's "three-inch golden lotuses" were considered aesthetically desirable. This practice was especially dominant in traditionally oriented families. So when my nineteen-year- old grandmother walked through the Gao family gate with her big feet, it became a matter of great curiosity and dissension within the household. Not only did people talk about her big feet, her strange accent was also a topic of discussion. People also noticed that she honored the Buddha with a ritual not usually seen in Chinese families.

Some well-traveled people concluded that this strange girl with the atypical surname "Jing" was not a Han Chinese person. She clearly came from another tribe! My grandmother came from a Tibetan sect in the town of Ganzi in Sichuan province, and her father was a Rinpoche within the Nyngma tradition of Tibetan Buddhism. The Nyngma tradition is considered the oldest sect of the four major branches of Tibetan Buddhism.

My grandmother's parents both died around the time she turned fifteen. From that point her father's Han Chinese disciple, who was a businessman, raised her. This disciple lived in Chengde near the Waiba Temple, which was run by lamas from Tibet and Mongolia. On a business trip to Beijing he met Thousand-Hectare Gao, and a marriage was arranged between my grandmother and Gao's son, who was to become my grandfather.

After their marriage, my grandmother was given a Han Chinese name: "Gao Jing." Not many people knew that her original name was Yeshe Tsuomu, meaning "Ocean of Wisdom."

Due to grandmother's influence, grandfather became interested in Vajrayana Buddhism.[3] By 1949, the year the Communists overthrew the Nationalists, my grandparents had become the center of spiritual life within their community, and many people became their followers. Because of this, my grandfather was branded "ringleader of Buddhist reactionary forces" by the radical government and put to death in 1950.

From that point forward, my grandmother began to hide her spiritual life, and would no longer profess any religious belief. Nevertheless, many believers continued to seek her out for private teachings, calling her the Big-Footed Buddha.

My father, whose ancestral home is in the province of Shandong, can best be described as a scientific realist. Because he hails from a region that was one of the heartlands of the Communist revolution, he and many of his relatives are cadres within the government. My parents met while my mother was studying at the Beijing Film Academy, and quickly married.

My mother ranks fourth among her siblings, and according to the local Beijing expression, was called "Fourth Miss." She was my grandfather's favorite child, and so was exposed to rare spiritual teachings. After my parents were married, they lived with grandmother.

One day, grandmother happily approached my mother and proclaimed that a joyous event was on its way. One month later, my

---
[3] Vajrayana refers to the tantric form of Buddhism that is practiced in Tibet. Its aims are close to those of Mahayana (the bodhisattva ideal of enlightening all beings), but it emphasizes transforming karmic energies toward enlightenment, rather than mere severance and deliverance from affliction. Vajrayana is also called Mi-zong (in Chinese and Lamaism).

mother was pregnant with me. My grandmother told my mother: "You will have a girl!" During the time before technology could scan for the sex of the fetus, the only way to find out the baby's gender was to wait until birth. Indeed, many events have proven that my grandmother possessed supernatural insight.

During my mother's nine months of pregnancy, though she suffered the discomforts associated with a first birth, my grandmother was in a constant state of bliss. Around the time I was due to be born, my grandmother, in a state of ecstatic joy, departed from her usual silent ways and spoke to my mother of many things, one of them being that Manjusri Bodhisattva had told her to name the baby girl Yuan Miao. My illiterate grandmother wrote the two characters "Yuan Miao" on a piece of paper, and asked my mother to look them up in a dictionary. My mother discovered that Miao has many meanings, all associated with large bodies of water, oceans. Yuan means the beginning, the primordial source.

On the day that I was born, according to my father, my grandmother was excited and moved to tears. The doctor came late, so my grandmother delivered me with her own hands. Owing to this circumstance I was born directly into her embrace. Thus began our lifelong *teacher-disciple* bond that went beyond our blood relationship.

On the Wings of Phoenix Rising

My Grandma did not like taking pictures, and those we had were torn up by Red Guards during the Cultural Revolution. In this photograph taken with my Mother, I look like a boy.

— 2 —

Leaving Home at Age Three

My father has no religious beliefs, and he has a formidable temper. He is not particularly a fan of my grandmother, especially her charitable ways. When I was two, my brother was born. Even with the arrival of a grandson, my grandmother was steadfast in her loving devotion to me. This was especially unacceptable to my father, who chauvinistically favored boys over girls.

Something happened to me when I was three that deeply affected the rest of my life and was prophetic of things to come. One day my mother returned from her job as a radio announcer, bringing with her a large bag of candy. China in the early 1960s was undergoing severe economic difficulties, and we relied heavily on household rations distributed by the government. A bag of candy in those days was considered a luxury. Because of her excellent performance at work, my mother had received this very special reward.

My grandmother quietly divided this bag of red candy into several portions, and distributed them among our neighbors, keeping just a small portion for our house. When my father returned from work and found only a small portion of candy left, he became irate! Though he could not scream at my grandmother directly, he did lift his foot and kicked me with one of his heavy Korean War surplus boots. My strapping father, in his boots that looked like two small boats, landed a kick on my lower back that sent me "flying" across the room. I hit the floor and blacked out.

My mother screamed: "The child is dead," and started to cry.

That kick really did make me take flight... I felt myself fly over the tree in the front of my house, then over our roof, all the way toward the sky. Then I was lofted upon a cottony cloud until I came before a dignified lady. She was wearing traditional garb and holding a vase in her hand. She was not only beautiful, but had an air of compassion and grace. Speaking to me in a melodic voice, she told me, "When you are grown, come back with an empty vase, and I will teach you." After speaking these words, she disappeared. I felt everything spinning around me, and there was a cold sensation in my throat. I could hear my parents calling to me in the distance. Then I opened my eyes, and found myself in the arms of my grandmother. Looking on were the worried faces of my father and mother.

As it turned out, after I "died," my grandmother resuscitated me by chanting mantras. She fed me a spoonful of cinnabar in my mouth with an ear-digging spoon, and after an hour-long ordeal I came back to life. I did not cry or scream after I revived, but only remembered that I should go back to that old lady to learn something. Three days later, I scrounged up an empty ink container from somewhere, and walked out of our house with it.

At that time, my family lived in an agricultural commune that had many open wells. It sometimes happened that children fell into these wells and were not discovered until much later…when it was too late. My disappearance caused quite a scene in my neighborhood, with each available person looking down the wells for me in vain. Someone notified the public safety bureau, which in turn began interviewing people in the area. They finally located an old shopkeeper who had seen a small child carrying an empty bottle headed north, talking about going to school with an old woman. The adults finally found me sleeping on the doorstep of an old house. Some other children had taken away my bottle, and I could not go to school with the old lady, so there was nothing left to do but go to sleep.

My mother was saddened and distraught over this episode, saying to my grandmother, "she is already leaving home at such a young age, how will we control her when she gets older?"

My grandmother responded: "Normal people surely cannot control her—the heavens will! She will leave home someday, and run all over the world." I was only three at the time of the incident (I felt much older, but my entire family has confirmed that I was only three). Nevertheless, I have vivid recollections of those leather boots, of flying in the air, and of that kindly lady with the vase.

On the Wings of Phoenix Rising

Myself at age four, after I ran away carrying an ink bottle in my hand. Because of this episode, I was nicknamed "Pingping" ('bottle' in Chinese).

— 3 —

Fear of Death at Age Seven

I began school at a young age and, being tall, always stood out from all the other kids in kindergarten. My parents could not forget my episode of searching for the *old lady*, so they exaggerated my age by two years to get me into school, hoping to prevent future incidents.

An age gap of only a few months can mean a big difference in a child's ability to care for themselves, not to speak of being two years younger, as I was. At times I could not control myself during morning exercises, resulting in wet pants and a puddle at my feet. I still remember our homeroom teacher, Mrs. Zhang, drying my cotton pants over a heater. By the time I started third grade I had just turned seven.

My neighborhood at that time, a residential area for families associated with the Agricultural Studies Institute, was like a village with about ten or so families. We could see each other's cooking smoke, and such proximity created a close-knit and familial environment. At that time, relations between people were still very simple. Trust and communication between people came naturally. We lived in a red brick house with various fruit trees and plants in our yard. Every day, we would walk out of this village to go to school or work. Dusk was the most exciting time of the day, when everyone returned to the village. The laughter of children filled the sky, and an air of felicity surrounded us.

Grandpa Zhang was a well-dressed old man with a long beard. He was the oldest person in the neighborhood, and accordingly, everyone called him "Grandpa." Grandpa Zhang liked to walk around the neighborhood, and we often heard the sound of his walking stick tapping the ground, *"tick, tick."* Because of his gracious disposition, he was loved by the whole neighborhood.

Coming home from school one day, I knew by the look on people's faces that something serious had happened. Grandma told me, "Grandfather Zhang died. Do you dare to go see him?" My father disapproved and wanted me to stay home, thinking it would be traumatic for me. Grandma said, "No need to be afraid. Go and have a look."

I squeezed through the crowd forming outside the Zhang house, and saw Grandpa Zhang lying motionless on the bed. His face was pale, and a strangely colored silk sheet covered him. He did not appear to be in any pain... perhaps he was just asleep. I was not afraid; in fact, I was very curious about the whole situation. Then the adults brought in a big wooden box, and I saw them put Grandpa Zhang in the big box. I began to get nervous when people put a big lid on this box. That lid appeared very heavy and it covered his whole body. What was going to happen when Grandpa Zhang woke, and was not strong enough to lift the lid? How could they do this? I almost screamed in protest.

The adults continued working methodically, nailing the lid shut. Every loud thud of the hammers fell on my youthful heart and spirit, *"dang dang."* I began to cry. How could these adults who seemed so courteous and kind to Grandpa Zhang go crazy like this? Even the family of Grandpa Zhang, his son, daughter-in-law and grandchildren, were part of this madness. Aside from the redness in their eyes from crying, they stood around as if nothing had happened, calmly greeting the numerous people that came by. No one seemed concerned with how Grandpa Zhang was feeling in that wooden box. I felt myself engulfed by the darkness that surrounded Grandpa Zhang, as if I were nailed inside with him.

Cremations were still uncommon back then, so Grandpa Zhang's body was delivered to the nearest cemetery by the whole procession. Curiously enough, I stood by and watched this whole process without any adult saying, "What are you doing here," or "No kids allowed." I began to watch the adults dig a hole, and some were even telling jokes while they dug the earth. When the hole was completed, they lowered the coffin into the ground with shouts of *"one, two, three"* and quickly covered it up with earth. I thought to myself, this is completely hopeless now. Poor Grandpa Zhang, who always took special pride in being clean, will never get out of this... he will become part of the dirt.

When the people were finished, they leisurely strolled back home.

It was late by the time I got home. An overwhelming fear and despair engulfed me, and I began to cry uncontrollably. My father continuously blamed my grandmother for allowing me to see a dead person, but she just chanted syllables in a strange language, which did calm me down a little.

That midnight, my mind returned to that lonely graveyard and with great pity I viewed the expressionless face and frozen body of Grandpa Zhang lying in that coffin. For several nights in a row, I experienced insomnia for the first time. Each night felt interminable as I covered my head in the blanket and quietly cried.

Why do people die? Can people not die?

For quite some time after that experience, I lived near the valley of death. My memories of Grandpa Zhang in that coffin haunted me—I was afraid of death!

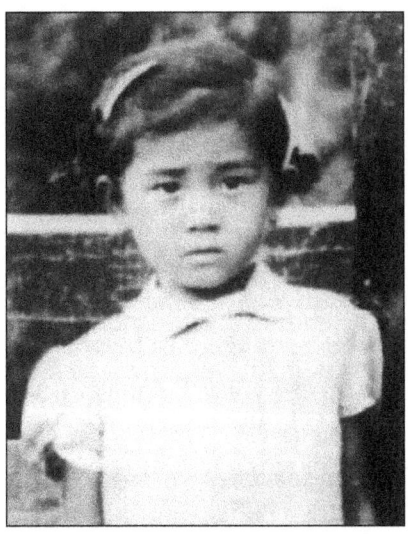

After witnessing Grandpa Zhang's burial, my face often wore this kind of expression.

— 4 —

Taking a Life at Age Ten

My home often had many small animals, usually rabbits and chickens.

When I turned ten, China was at the height of the Cultural Revolution and things became chaotic at my school. The cry to "quit school and rebel" led our school to close down. With time on my hands, I turned my attention to nurturing little animals.

Of all the animals I've had, a little white chicken comes to mind the most. She had a pretty comb and walked regally with head erect and chest puffed out among the milling, pecking flock. Her appearance and bearing were nothing like an ordinary chicken. I even gave her a name, calling her my little "White Egret."

White Egret was very smart, and related well to people. She had a pair of very clear and tender black eyes, and when she looked at me, I always felt there there was a hundred things she wanted to tell me.

At that time, because of political problems connected with my grandfather, and grandmother's unwillingness to acknowledge "guilt," the Red Guards sent her away to a rural commune for reeducation and punishment. I missed her very much, and often shared my thoughts with little White Egret.

"Come over here," I would call out to her. She would jump on my leg, raise her little head, and stare at me with those deep black eyes. "Wouldn't it be great if you were a pigeon who could deliver letters to Grandma?" White Egret would cluck shyly, expressing her regrets.

Even as I stared dreamily into the sky, she would be by my side, daydreaming along with me. At night when I gasped in amazement at the sight of a meteor, she too would murmur in surprise. And when I cried from missing Grandma so much, she even pecked at my teardrops as though she wanted to taste my tears.

One day a friend visited me and noticed my friendship with White Egret. He laughed at the treatment I gave a simple farm chicken, for he had a real bird that could fly!

Not too long after, he brought that bird over to show me. I don't recall exactly what kind of bird that was, just that he called it "Flying Brother." Flying Brother was well trained indeed, and had mastered several tricks. With effortless flaps of its wings, it took flight and landed at its master's command. The sight of this bird was an affront to my vanity, and I was jealous.

I called for White Egret and fed her, then clutched her in my hands. She struggled in my grasp, not knowing what I wanted her to do. Unwilling to be outdone by anyone, I threw her into the sky with all my strength. White Egret screamed, fluttered her wings, and landed in a lopsided manner—I had killed her!

I was filled with remorse, realizing that I had killed this lovely and blameless little spirit. I placed her little body in a wooden box, and buried her with a caption on her wooden plaque, stating: "White Egret, I've wronged you!" This was my first lesson on the effects of jealousy and vanity. Though there have been other lessons since, this was the most memorable one.

I am writing this with repentance, to say I am sorry to all living things that I have harmed either knowingly or unknowingly.

I am sorry to all living things that I have harmed, either knowingly or unknowingly. This picture was taken in Xiantong Temple at Wutai Mountain.

— 5 —

My First Love

In college I was a bashful, reticent girl and did not like noisy gatherings. What was more, I was still the youngest and tallest among my classmates, just as in middle school and grade school.

For college-age kids, in the springtime of their youth, falling in love is a natural experience. I began to notice other girls going out excitedly to meet with boys. On such occasions, their faces would be flushed, and their voices tender. Even those who were normally outspoken and assertive seemed to exude a sweet demeanor when they were in love.

I majored in the humanities, and there was a shortage of tall boys in my class. In fact, there were not many tall boys in my entire major. Friends joked with me, saying I should major in physical education because those boys would not be afraid of me, and being taller, would not have to look up at me during conversations.

You can say that I was pretty "clueless" when it came to boys. Sometimes boys would come to my dorm room under one auspice or another. During those times, I would not feel very involved or interested in conversation and would sometimes leave the room altogether. Coming back, I was often chastised by my roommate for being rude: "I think he was here to see you, but you ran off.". But under that veil, I had romantic dreams like everyone else. I yearned to have a brilliant young man by my side.

It finally happened around my third year in college—I had "feelings" for a certain boy. He was an outstanding young man, a Mongolian who had grown up in the interior of China. Not only was he talented at singing and dancing, he was also good at telling humorous stories.

I played center on our department's girl's basketball team, and he was student body president, so we had many occasions to meet as he escorted our team to various competitions. We gradually got to know each other. Even after the basketball season ended, he would come and visit me in class. He was open, down to earth, and would always look directly at me. His stares embarrassed me and filled my heart with sweetness at the same time. I wanted to see him, and was at the same time afraid to see him. That was the experience of my first love.

One day, he sent me a letter, saying that although he had planned not to date anyone until graduation, he could no longer wait… "The summer is almost upon us; will you join me on the Mongolian plains? I would like to teach you horseback riding." I was deeply touched by this letter, and counted the days before summer vacation.

One early morning, a little more than one month before summer vacation, I was startled out of sleep. I saw him dressed in white, standing before me in the darkness. He had a sad expression on his face, and his eyes were red from crying.

I asked him "Why are you crying?"

He answered, " I want to hold your hand..." I extended my hand to him, and then he disappeared into thin air.

This dreamlike experience disturbed me, and I got out of bed early. I waited anxiously for the morning bell to ring, so I could see him if possible during morning drill. Strangely enough, the morning bell never rang. My roommate who loved to stay in bed said happily, "I hope it's like this every day." But an ominous feeling crept over me.

Finally, after nine in the morning, the shocking news came. At four in the morning, Student Wang had suffered a heart attack; emergency measures were taken to no avail, and he was dead. This news was met with much wailing from members of the student body. The janitor responsible for the morning bell was the saddest. This lonely old man said the boy had been the kindest and humblest of all the students he had encountered. Many young people were selfish and showed no regard for others, but this young man had often helped with janitorial chores, never showing a trace of arrogance.

I did not cry out loud, but only sobbed to myself...

This is how my first love ended.

Yuan Miao

The sweetness of young love once filled my heart.

— 6 —

My Uncle

My grandmother's main method of teaching was through direct oral transmission. Because she could not read or write, she did not rely on books for her source of knowledge and power. This mode of teaching is a feature associated with the Nyngma and Geluk traditions of Tibetan Buddhism. Grandma's enlightenment songs and mantras came flowing straight from her inner nature. She always expressed her realizations gained from deep meditative states in a straightforward and direct manner.

I like this method of transmission and teaching very much because of its liveliness, flexibility, and power of personal confirmation. When she sent me at age seven to watch the burial of Grandpa Zhang, she was actually giving me an important lesson in life—the realization of mortality. This is an important component of all Tibetan teaching lineages.

Only by understanding death and being familiar with death can one comprehend the impermanent, phantasmal nature of life. This is crucial for overcoming mental attachment and all the resulting forms of ignorance. I now realize that all my experiences with death along my path were not coincidences, but were guided by Heaven.

Grandma taught me to penetrate the mystery of life and death, and her life experience illustrated all varieties of death and separation from loved ones. When she was fifteen years old, both her parents died in quick succession. Her father—my great grandfather—was a Rinpoche of the Tibetan Nyngma order, and a lifelong devotee of the great Tibetan adept Milarepa. Among Tibetan traditions, Milarepa represents the practical dharma. In his teaching he dispensed with rigid and complex philosophies and placed emphasis on practical cultivation and direct experience. As a result, many people place Milarepa alongside the Sixth Patriarch Hui Neng of Chan Buddhism, because their teachings emphasize practice as opposed to theoretical discussions. Many people have accepted their teachings because of their special ability to make spiritual truths accessible. From a young age Grandma was trained in forbearance, devotion to practice, and non-attachment to material comforts.

Grandma had seven children, two of them sons.

In 1950, because of my grandfather's strong appeal as a spiritual leader, he was put on trial by the radical government as a "Buddhist reactionary ringleader." Prior to his execution, Grandma was given one last chance to visit him, and my grandfather told her, "One of our descendants will become enlightened. You must take good care of this special one..."

Another tragedy preceded Grandpa's execution: my third uncle, the first-born son of my grandparents, died of a sudden heart attack at the tender age of twelve. Within a short few months, Grandma lost both her husband and a son. After this tragic chapter, she entered a period of long silence.

Though I never met my third uncle or my grandfather, I knew that Grandma loved them dearly. She told me: "The way of Buddha is the way of salvation. Your grandfather was not a reactionary. Compassion was what he cherished, and he came to this world to spread the Buddha's teachings. Your uncle belongs to the realm of heavenly beings. He came to earth to experience suffering, and when his karma was resolved, he ascended to higher realms."[4]

Every time Grandma gave me these deep explanations, I would gaze at the transcendent light radiating from her eyes.

Mother also had a younger brother, my grandma's youngest son, whom my mother called "Old Little Brother." In colloquial Beijingese, "Old" means the youngest and dearest. My "little" uncle's name was Gao Yutang. He used to play with me when I was little, but as his schoolwork grew demanding, I saw less of him. While I was attending elementary school, he went to college. During his sophomore year he was diagnosed with severe heart disease, so he left school to nurse his health. I was happy to have him stay with us, and he was like a second father to me.

Grandma taught Uncle and me how to sit in meditation and recite a few mantras. She also taught Uncle some special techniques, such as Vajrayana hand mudras and body mudras.

During the height of the "red scare" of the Cultural Revolution, Grandma was hauled off by Red Guards to the countryside, and Uncle stayed with my family under the care of my mother.

---

4 Buddhists believe in six planes of transmigration (devas, asuras, humans, beasts, hungry ghosts, and hell-dwellers), of which the deva realm is the highest. But the deva realm is still not the highest plane in the multidimensional universe.

There was a special bond between Mother and Uncle. One day I overheard them talking: Uncle was worried that he might not have long to live, and was worried that Grandma could not bear it. He asked my mother to console her when it happened. My poor mother tried her best to keep Uncle healthy.

Before long, Uncle asked to be near Grandma. He went to Grandma's side, and it was in her arms that he breathed his last breath. Every midnight of the three days prior to his departure, a translucent white-clad old man came into Uncle's room. Uncle gave specific instructions to have a chair placed by his bed for the visitor. The old man was a messenger from Heaven. On the third day at midnight, this messenger took Uncle with him back to Heaven.

Grandma oversaw all the details of my uncle's funeral, then returned to her normal peaceful ways. Seeing such inexplicable composure, my father was beside himself, for he too dearly loved my uncle. After Uncle's death, my father was depressed and grieved. He simply could not understand how a mother could be calm after the death of a son.

"I never want to hear her talk about things like goodness and evil. She is too cruel! Her own flesh and blood is dead, and I don't see a trace of sadness in her. Her heart must be made of stone," I would hear my father muttering to himself and others. But I distinctly recall seeing Grandma during meditation, calling out Uncle's name with trembling lips. I saw her many nights in the moonlight making prostrations, praying and chanting. Those images of Grandma's sorrowful expression, showing the burden of her years, will forever be etched in my heart.

Even today I often recall that scene and wonder if a seeker or enlightened person can really be unmoved by ties of feeling? Through my own experience I recognize that "an ardent mind is the Buddha-mind." One who is close to Truth does not distance herself from friends and family. At home she should be the best of parents, the best of spouses. She should be the best child to her own parents. Being true to her incarnated form, she possesses the full spectrum of human feelings. At the passing of her loved ones, she feels genuine sorrow and loss. But ultimately sorrow heightens her sense of impermanence and propels her toward awakening. In light of the Buddha-nature, she uplifts and transcends these ties of feeling, making them resources on the way to realization.

This was my young Uncle at the time of his illness. Grandma said, "Your uncle belongs to the realm of heavenly beings. He came to earth to experience suffering, and when his karma was resolved, he ascended to higher realms..."

— 7 —

Peony in Springtime

On every birthday or special occasion since my birth, Grandma would conduct a secret ceremony for me. She would write out *dharani*[5] inscriptions on paper and burn them, then dissolve the ashes in water and ask me to drink them. The inscriptions were as foreign to me as words written on celestial scrolls. I have drunk potions made from drawings of constellations, geometrical mandalas, and totems. During these proceedings, care was taken to make the ceremony solemn, and I was not supposed to act frivolously.

On one occasion, I thoughtlessly quipped, "Other kids eat cake and light candles for their birthdays, but I celebrate mine by lighting incense and drinking ashes. How funny!" That day when I drank the ash water, I did not follow Grandma's instruction to drink the entire cup in one gulp, but instead swallowed it in several sips. A few minutes later my eyes swelled up, and I lost my voice. After that

---

5 Dharani are one type of mantra; they are words of power that are chanted or written for healing or protective purposes.

incident, I became more mindful of my speech.

Such was the juxtaposition of the physical and the metaphysical that I grew up under: The external me received a modern scientific education and had a fashionable career, while the inner me was connected to the timeless spiritual universe.

Grandma forbade me to seek out fortune tellers, and she also frowned on people telling my fortune by physiognomy. Nevertheless, due to the nature of my profession, I came into contact with people from all walks of life. It was hard to avoid meeting people who wanted to get a psychic fix on me.

All of the many fortune tellers who volunteered their services gave me favorable "readings." On three separate occasions, the phrase "peony in springtime" was used to describe me.

Looking back on my life, and leaving out the deaths of loved ones, my life did indeed fit the profile of a "peony in springtime."[6] Ever since I can remember, in my career and personal life, things have often come together according to my wishes.

Beginning with my primary schooling, I was always the teacher's pet. Though I did not pursue my studies vigorously, I always placed among the top few places in examinations. Every time there were recruiting efforts for roles in stage productions or membership on sports teams, I was always the first choice. The outcome of these activities, however, was a different story, since I often performed awkwardly due to shyness.

I don't know how it happened, but I won a place on a citywide gymnastics team. I remember that our weekly practice was on Sunday afternoon. One day when I was running late, Grandma put a

---

6 Peonies are a traditional symbol of wealth and prestige in China. "Peony in springtime" is an image for one who enjoys material blessings.

few handfuls of peanuts in my pocket to eat if I got hungry. By the time I rushed to the gym, the others had already started warming up. The coach told me to hustle, saying, "Do your warm-ups and change later," so I started jumping up and down in my regular street clothes...*one, two, three.*

As I was jumping around, a strange popping sound could be heard under my feet. Looking down I realized the crunching came from the peanuts falling out of my pockets. I quickly bent down to pick up my snack, causing all my teammates to laugh and the coach to scold me angrily. Without saying anything, I quietly picked up all the peanuts and left the gym.

One of the things that Grandma taught me was to cherish blessings. Though she would not spare any expense to assist others, she was always very frugal in her own habits. Even if a grain of rice fell to the floor, she would have me pick it up, telling me that even a king should treat a grain of rice as something precious. Only a kind-hearted king would know how difficult it was for each grain of rice to reach his table. If that was the case with a single grain of rice, imagine handfuls of peanuts!

When Grandma heard about my experience at the gym, she laughed so hard her eyes watered. She exclaimed: "That's great, that's great! After all, your destiny was never to become some kind of actor or athlete."

"Then what should I do?" was my natural response. She became silent for a while, and then said, "You should not be in the business of performing or acting. You must come and go as you truly are. In acting you would need to put on make-up, and that is the exact opposite of what you must do. Aside from that, you will not be in a field that requires competition. You must not be competitive or concerned about winning. You don't have the gift or the need to pursue such things. The things that you will be doing..." Stopping here, she gestured toward the heavens with a mudra, and said, "You will know when you are grown up!"

Ever since my grade school years, I have had an affinity for teaching. Even then, whenever a lower grade needed a temporary teacher, I was always the one appointed to such tasks. I would stand before the class, feeling inadequate but imitating a teacher's tones as I taught students almost my own age to read from their lesson books.

As it happened in later years, I did serve a stint as a teacher. Prior to my career as a television director, I taught at both the high school and college levels.

In 1984, I suddenly became interested in becoming a television reporter and director. In less than a year, I began working for Chinese Central Television (CCTV).

Quickly following my debut as a director, my second documentary won a major prize in the highest national awards event. Suddenly, I received widespread recognition as a "talented female director" on her way up. My superiors at the network had high hopes for me to develop on all fronts, and even wanted me to consider becoming a program host.

Wherever I went in China doing interviews and shooting footage, my crew and I were always received hospitably by the highest-ranking local officials, who were sure to heap praise on me: "We are honored that Central Broadcasting has sent one of its best directors..." After hearing enough of such remarks, I treated them as routine pleasantries. From 1995 to 1998, I went on film-making trips to Europe and Australia. It was there that I discovered that people were describing me as a talented documentary filmmaker. When the Norwegian national media covered our filming activities, my crew even teased me for being on the verge of "international stardom."

Chinese Central Television is a well-funded "super station" with an abundance of talent on its staff. Calling it a super station is not an exaggeration, considering that it has the world's largest television audience (250 million households), and a staff of tens of thousands. CCTV is China's highest official media organ, and my dual credentials as reporter and director for CCTV brought me respect and hospitality wherever I went in China.

By the time I came to America, CCTV had a total of nine channels, and the first channel was known as the golden channel. Prime time on this channel was known as "golden time," due to the large number of viewers and the advertising rates it commanded.

I worked on two famous programs broadcast during this "golden time." One program was "Splendors of Cathay," and another was "People and Nature." As a result, the name Yuan Miao became known to large numbers of television viewers.

The saying has it that "forebears plant the tree, and descendants enjoy the shade." Because of what was passed down by my forebears, along with my savings from years of directing work, before coming to America I was considered materially well off by Chinese standards.

Finding myself with material abundance that had come to me unsought, I never forgot Grandma's admonishment: "A peony stands for wealth, but it belongs to this world only. You have to be like a lotus, born from the mud but unstained. In this way, you will not lose your home in heaven."

After coming to America, karmic conditions allowed me to live in a beautiful new house. But conditions rise and conditions fade, so I moved from that new house to a small room in San Gabriel. Living there for a period of six months, I experienced an expansiveness and fulfillment of spirit that I had not known before. Later, new conditions arose to let me enter a solitary retreat in Malibu, overlooking the Pacific Ocean and encircled by beautiful mountain scenery.

My past and current spiritual mentors, in their love for me, have watched over me from behind the scenes, freeing me from worry so I may cultivate myself quietly and carry out Heaven's work.

The external me received a modern education and had a fashionable career, while the inner me was still connected to the timeless spiritual universe.

— 8 —

Seventh Month of the Year 1985

After graduating from college and entering my profession, I grew lackadaisical in my spiritual practice. Especially after becoming a director, my days were taken up with the ins and outs of a high-status position. I was on top of the world, and my head was spinning. Grandma's teachings simply felt too distant from my reality at the time, and my fashionable, fulfilling profession fueled my vanity. I was smartly attired, confident and proud. This continued up to 1985, which proved to be a fateful year for me.

That year my fortunes in worldly affairs were for the most part excellent. My career was going well, and good luck seemed to be at my beck and call. I was a married woman then, and because my husband's work was as busy as mine, I left my three-year-old daughter in the care of my mother. Many times I regretted not spending more time with my daughter. So I took her for a summer holiday at the seashore on Qinhuang Island. For a week we spent our vacation swimming, walking, and enjoying a peaceful time together. One night my daughter awoke from her sleep said she had dreamt of her Great-Grandma. That same night, I too had a dream about Grandma.

Longing for Grandma overtook me, so much that I decided to cut short the holiday to visit Grandma. Feeling as though we were being ushered by invisible forces to be near her, we left the seaside immediately. That was the day of the full moon, on the 15th of the Seventh Month.

Grandma was living with Third Aunt, and Mother was there as well. After arriving there in the evening, I went to bed. Mother and Aunty stayed up chatting quietly, and Grandma was off in another room. Though my trip had been hectic, I was not tired in the least. Instead I had an inexplicable feeling of excitement.

Suddenly, a bright ray of light streaked before my eyes. I opened my eyes widely, and saw a shining orange globe outside my window. I immediately turned to look out the other window so I could see it from another angle. A bright-silver full moon shone high in the sky, and right outside the window was that globe of light.

"Why did you hang a lantern outside, Aunty?" I asked. I heard Mother and Third Aunt reply at the same time: "What lantern, what you are seeing must be the moon!"

"No, outside the large window," I responded.

Mother and Aunty jumped up from their beds and looked intently for the globe, but saw nothing. As I stared intently into the globe, a small voice sounded in my ear: "Go ask Grandma…" So with Mother and Auntie's help, Grandma dressed and came out of her room. By then the globe had divided into several smaller globes of light, and was now dispersed throughout my visual field on the roof, trees, and outside the window.

After burning incense, bowing and chanting mantras, Grandma called forth a sacred vision. In a field of light, my Grandma, Yeshe Tsuomu, merged with high masters to give me empowerment. I was anointed and favored with revelations. It was a wonderfully sacred and solemn moment, so moving that tears streamed down both cheeks. The Compassionate Guanyin, Manjusri, Amitabha, the white-clad messenger who had come for my Uncle, the angel who had come for me, and Green Tara—all these came to cleanse my eyes and give me revelations.

My aunt who was watching with fleshly eyes fearfully stood off to one side and merely asked favors for her two sons, hoping that one might find gainful employment and the other a good wife.

The following day, the sixteenth of the seventh month, was beautifully sunny until a lightning storm broke out at dusk. Amid the sound of thunder, two golden dragons descended onto Grandma's house. Neighbors who witnessed the sight were amazed... Almost simultaneously, another phenomenon occurred at my mother's house 170 kilometers away—an oppressive feeling was in the air, and then a large globe of light descended from the sky, to the sound of thunder. It entered our house and then dispersed into numerous smaller globes, which flew into a neighbor's house, shorting out a television set and refrigerator. Our elderly neighbor was so frightened that he hid under his bed, and my father was stunned as well.

On the third day, several kids playing in the neighborhood saw "flying people" wearing colorful clothing above Grandma's home.

As for me, I fell into a paranormal state unlike anything in my experience. My first impression was that the world had changed. Everything I trained my sight on was revealed to be other than what it seemed. Then came waves of compassion that extended to the smallest living things: bees, birds, butterflies all became objects of great sympathy. Even my body experienced changes: waves of heat spread through my body, and I felt the urge to run, jump and spin freely in nature. Sometimes when sitting down for a meal, a great force would pull me away and send me out spinning in great circles. This state persisted for three months, requiring me to take a leave of absence to weather this period.

Later, whenever I entered a meditative state, my body naturally manifested various movements.[7] The majority of these were done on the ground, quite unlike the standing movements of traditional Chinese *qigong*.

Father became very worried and believed I was developing psychological problems. Mother on the other hand understood, for she had witnessed the events that began this process.

My movements became more numerous and nuanced, to the point that on our daily walks to the park, Mother and Brother brought along a blanket to prepare for my "ground movements." According to their observations and notes, I performed dozens of movements while in this state of self-tempering, none of which were similar to commonly seen *qigong* forms. Since then these naturally revealed postures and body mudras, empowered and selected by various high masters, have become the *Nine Steps of Yoga of Joy*.

The Seventh Month of 1985—that time so close to me yet so distant! Now, finally, I can get it off my chest. So much has been transformed over sixteen years, so many reversals have happened.

I have strayed and retreated and wavered, to the disappointment

---

[7] For an explanation of the principle behind this, see "Return to True Nature" on page 175.

of my high masters. Thinking of how my obstinate nature has hindered my self-cultivation leaves me with unending regret.

Following the Seventh Month of 1985, I began experimenting with yogic postures.

— 9 —

An Unintentional Vow

After the seventh month of 1985, non-physical mentors frequently visited me. I would sometimes be awakened from sleep by light, and in the light was that kindly lady I had seen at age three. She was the Prajna Buddha-Mother, also an emanation of Guanyin Bodhisattva. I would then fall "asleep" and be shown visions and be given guidance. Later on in my studies I found that these experiences, in Buddhist terms, were examples of *Guru Yoga* and *Dream Yoga*. The practice of Guru Yoga and Dream Yoga gave me strong faith and incomparable devotion.

Another yogic means to align with the high masters is by information sent through embodied persons with whom one has an affinity.

The elder Wu Zhenfa was a renowned doctor of Chinese medicine in his seventies. Additionally, he was a devoted cultivator whose years of Chan meditation had given him special insight. One day during his meditation practice, he suddenly had an impulse to take a walk in the park. So he rose from his cushion and went to the park, where he saw me meditating. He watched for a few moments, then struck up a conversation with me. The second time we met was when he came to my home, on his own initiative, to expound the *Heart Sutra* and *Diamond Sutra* for me. Prior to this, I had very little exposure to Buddhist sutras.

Old Mr. Wu was a gifted teacher, and I brought my notes from our session to America with me. In addition to teaching me these two sutras, he encouraged me to become invulnerable to the "Eight Winds" of gain, loss, favor, resentment, slander, fame, honor, and humiliation.

In hindsight, for one of little wisdom like myself, my extra-physical encounters created new ego obstacles for me. For a long time I seemed to float above the world, and my outlook was very naive. Though not lacking in faith and devotion, I was nevertheless poorly equipped for the path of cultivation. Though I appreciated old Mr. Wu's wisdom, at the same time I thought: "I am not an ordinary person: the gods will protect me. Even the gods are on my side. I am not afraid of those eight winds."

Around the same time, another distant uncle in his seventies came to visit from afar. He was a close disciple of my grandfather who had not visited us for more than thirty years. Grandfather had come to him in a dream and requested him to visit "Fourth Miss"— my mother. After searching for some time, he finally found us.

This uncle was very devout, and had been in the inner circle of Grandfather's followers. In spite of his advanced years, he still made one hundred full prostrations every morning and prayed single-mindedly. Because of his continued practice, he appeared quite healthy and serene. This uncle lived with us for three months, observing me wordlessly all the while. Just before his departure, he told that Grandfather had made a prophecy that *so-and-so* would be incarnated in a number of years. In fact, this uncle believed that I was the person in the prophecy. He also instructed me to observe secrecy in such matters and to follow Heaven's wish in all I did. I should be ready to "climb a mountain of knives and plunge into a sea of fire." If the goal is to save all beings, there is no room for selfishness.

This uncle's devotion left a deep impression on me. After this meeting I referred to all devout Tibetan rinpoches as uncles. Even to Losang Rinpoche, a living Buddha of the Gelugpa sect, I gave the nickname "Uncle Rinpoche." Uncle Rinpoche's written work, entitled *Love: An Eruption of Heart-Wisdom*, is an excellent book. More on this matter will be found in the Chapter 17, *"A Glorious Procession of Rinpoches."*

One night my holy father,[8] Manjusri Bodhisattva, appeared before me. With a thunderous voice he asked: "There are two roads, one is smooth and surrounded by flowers, the other rugged, narrow and barren. The latter, however, leads to Heaven and can save human beings. Which do you chose?" Almost without thinking I told him that I chose the latter.

"Can you make the needed sacrifices?" he asked. My response was just as quick: "Of course! I am willing to renounce both fame and fortune toward the higher goal." I said all this with complacency, as though I were truly living up to my great spiritual potential.

Inadvertently, I had entered into a very substantial contract with the heavens. Later, to fulfill this promise, I sacrificed my dearest "flower" in the world—my daughter. I would have to continue climbing

---

[8] The author received her name from Manjusri Bodhisattva, so she calls him Holy Father.

alone and out of the world's view.

There have been times when I severely regretted making this irresponsible vow. In my fits of outrage I wished to enter a "celestial court" to seek justice. But in fact once you make a serious vow, there is no running away or turning back.

Have you ever made an ultimate vow?

On the Wings of Phoenix Rising

For one of little wisdom like myself, my extra-physical encounters created new ego obstacles for me. For a long time I seemed to float above the world, and my outlook was very naive.

Inadvertently, I had entered into a very substantial contract with the heavens. Later, to fulfill this promise, I sacrificed my dearest "flower" in the world—my daughter. I would have to continue climbing alone and out of the world's view.

— 10 —

Those "Poor Monks"... Why Are They So Poor?

After old Mr. Wu expounded the *Heart Sutra* and *Vajra Sutra* for me, I not only became interested in various sutras and texts but also developed a fascination with temples and the lives of renunciates.

I thought to myself that if Grandma, who was just an ordinary person, knew so much and had such power, those "professional" adepts must be something! Also, Grandma's purely oral style of transmission was no longer sufficient to satisfy my thirst for knowledge, so I decided to visit various temples for a master with greater ability. Grandma had admonished me not to seek out a master deliberately: "When the Dharma is in decline, it is difficult to separate the false from the real...one must follow the course that was meant to be..." But I could not restrain my curiosity and was determined to find out for myself.

In 1988, I visited Guangji Temple in Beijing. Because this was the home to the Chinese Buddhist Association, I thought this was a place of "crouching tigers and hidden dragons," where a great adept might be found. Sure enough, as I entered the temple, I was accosted by a spare-featured old monk. He laughingly said to me: "You are meant to be here…It's just in time for tomorrow…You're going to be initiated!" I found his approach refreshing, and thought that after all these years it was about time to be taking refuge.[9]

The following morning I arrived early at the temple with gifts in hand and, under the guidance of this monk, took part in a solemn Refuge Ceremony. I was excited, because taking refuge made me an "official" disciple of Buddhism.

I told Grandma about this formality, and she told me to visit the temple again the following month on the 15th day of the lunar calendar. For this visit to the temple I took along even more fruits, delicacies, and flowers than before, almost filling up my car. Upon entering the temple, I noticed two "Red Banner" sedans parked in the courtyard. This model of car was only for use by the exclusive few who held high-level positions.

Passing through the second gate I arrived at the monks' quarters and came to the door of my "master." I heard loud and excited speech inside the room, and the monk appeared to be in high spirits. I knocked on the door.

Five people were already sitting inside, and the monk immediately and proudly identified them as the passengers of those privileged cars parked outside. An older lady among them gave me a self-assured smile. "Obviously, these guests require no introduction,

---

9 'Taking refuge' is an initiation, similar to a baptism, in which one accepts the Triple Jewels of the Buddhist faith: the Buddha (the awakened one), dharma (law of awakening), and sangha (community of seekers).

and you know their status... Even *they* are my disciples... Can you believe that I have already visited the Statehouse twice?" He then introduced me to the group: "Here is my new initiate. She has a good root of wisdom and is an up-and-coming journalist..."

The entire scene made me feel as if cold water had been poured on my head. I felt misled. Having sought by all means to leave the noisy pursuit of fame and profit, I hardly expected that in this hallowed temple, the clamor would be even more strident.

Dejectedly I returned home to Grandma's side. She did not ask me anything, but only repeated a saying: "One year after taking monastic orders, the Buddha is before your eyes; two years after, the Buddha is on the horizon; three years after, the Buddha is nowhere to be found..."

Not wanting to leave it at that, I kept searching. My next destination was Beijing Fayuan Temple—home of the China Buddhist Institute. This time I would change my approach, for I no longer wished to take refuge with anyone. I asked a Chan master named Bai-guang if I could audit classes together with young monastics. Bai-guang introduced me to an instructor of Buddhist *vinaya*[10] and made my request known to him.

This old monk rejected my request on the grounds that a lay female cannot attend class with male monks. I assured them that I understood and graciously took leave, offering my card along with a small donation. Apparently my card had an effect, because the instructor made an exception for me and arranged for me to audit the course from the back row.

During this period as auditor in the Buddhist Institute, I came

---

10 Vinaya is the Buddhist code of rules and precepts that are taught in a catechistic manner to monastic initiates.

in contact with the young monks there. Some of them were indeed following the monastic regimen because of a sincere search for truth. Others had to leave lay life for reasons ranging from failed romance or economic hardship to physiological problems. Later I made a documentary film titled "The China Buddhist Institute," in which I depicted this top institution of Buddhist higher learning, which turns out temple abbots and dharma masters.

After the film was shown on CCTV, I received some letters from viewers wanting to know more about how they could actually leave lay life and enroll at the China Buddhist Institute. In a written response, I replied to one viewer: "Do you know what is entailed? You would merely be leaving your worldly 'home' and entering the larger 'home' of the monastery. Ask yourself what exactly is implied in the idea of 'home'? Must Truth and home be mutually exclusive?"

After my desire to seek a master subsided, I had the occasion to visit Meizhou Island off Fujian Province, to film a program at the birthplace of the Ocean Goddess *Ma-zu*.[11] I met an old nun in a seaside temple who was worth getting to know. I could not understand a word of her earthy Min-nan dialect, but there was no mistaking what was in her heart—it was filled with unstained compassion and penetrating wisdom about human life. Living in her small temple for a week, I ventured each day across a bridge to the seashore, where I meditated on a large boulder. The old nun and two generations of her disciples practiced their daily meditation there without regard for weather conditions. Their devotion and sincerity left a deep imprint on me.

Regarding those who have no more than half-digested book

---

11 Ma-zu is a goddess worshipped in folk temples along the Eastern Chinese seaboard. In popular belief she is the patron goddess of sea-faring people.

knowledge, but are lacking in right views and compassion, one of my masters commented sadly: "Why are they called *poor monks?*[12] What makes them poor? Because they are poor of heart..."

---

12 Chinese monks often refer to themselves as poor monks as a gesture of renunciation and meekness.

— 11 —

Grandma Goes Home

Yeshe Tsuomu, translated from Tibetan, means "Ocean of Wisdom." Although few knew the meaning of Grandma's name, she revealed a wisdom that won the praise of many. During the Cultural Revolution, because her late husband had been executed as a "reactionary Buddhist ringleader," and due to her own reputation as the "Big-Footed Buddha," she too was branded among the reactionary "five black types"[13] and banished to a country village to do menial farm labor. A number of zealous, pigheaded interrogators took turns subjecting her to "education" sessions trying to rid her of her faith-based world view.

Unfailingly, her only response to these abusive interrogations was a gentle smile and silence. Her smile radiated an inordinate amount of energy, and her crystal clear eyes were hard for some people to stare into.

---

13 An insulting term used during political persecutions of the Cultural Revolution, meaning that someone belongs to the five categories of despicable people.

"Gao with the Big Feet, shut your eyes, and wipe that smile off your face," one young man roared.

Sure enough, she stopped smiling, and became somber. She then quietly told the young man, "Your wife is about to give birth, and faces a difficult delivery. Only one life can be saved. Do you want to keep the adult or the infant?" This immediately stunned the young man and everyone there, since his wife's pregnancy was known only to a few, and certainly not to this woman under reeducation.

Later that night, that young man quietly snuck out to beg Grandma for her guidance. "Please, Big-Footed Grandma, I want the adult and the child both to live. Please bless this delivery."

To that Grandma replied: "You silly children, it's as though your hearts have been possessed by ghosts. The gods are high above in the heavens, and all your screaming and misbehaving will only sow bad karma for yourselves! I cannot help you. Only you can help yourself. Three days from now, take time off work to be by your wife's side when she gives birth, and refrain from doing more evil."

Sure enough the man's wife had a difficult delivery, but due to efforts made on her behalf, both the mother and infant survived. The man, however, died in a car accident two years later.

Grandma often said that in order to have vast wisdom, one must first possess great compassion. In fact, the measure of wisdom is directly related to measure of compassion. Although Grandma was virtually illiterate, I often discovered nuggets of profound illumination in her simple, humble ways.

In 1996, I gave Grandma a dragon-headed walking stick. This cane was made of peppertree wood, and the grip was an ornately carved dragon's head. One of the eyes worked as a flashlight, and the other eye activated a siren, in case she fell down while walking. Such a walking stick might come in handy for a woman in her nineties.

When I explained the functions of this gift to her, Grandma said, "Now that I have this stick, maybe I'll stray from the light and stumble into delusions...I will no longer have any courage." She had me hang this cane on the wall to be enjoyed as a painting.

Because Grandma had very little "feeling" for luxuries or material enjoyments, people who wished to provide for her had very few avenues for expression. In 1987 I bought some very nice bed linens and fitted her bed with them. Several days later, she put the old linens back in place. She said to me: "Fine things are just another hindrance. The smallest hindrance can be a burden. Your heart must be big, not wasted on such small matters."

The following year I gave her a black velvet hat designed for elders, adorned with a round piece of green jade. When she tried on this hat in front of the mirror, she said, "It's as though I have grown a head of black hair...it does make me look younger. When I take it off...I am still a bundle of impermanence."

In October 1989, Grandma came down with the flu and refused treatment. Seven days later while calmly asleep she entered nirvana, having lived for ninety-nine years.

Yuan Miao

My Grandma left this picture before she passed away. That day she herself suggested: "I want my picture taken."

— 12 —

Even My Daughter Is Gone

In the days after Grandma passed on to her heavenly home, I stayed silent and kept to myself. I developed a strong aversion to mundane life, and looked at the tumultuous world from an outsider's perspective. Even so, there was still tenderness in my life because I had a daughter.

My daughter's name was Yuan Liyuan—a name given by my heavenly patriarch when she was two. Grandma had told me that the "little angel" was to be renamed, and Manjusri Bodhisattva later revealed her name to us.

Liyuan was pretty and intelligent—truly a lovely little girl whom many people adored. Early in my pregnancy, Guanyin Bodhisattva appeared and told me, "This child is a gift to you…" I then described to her what I wanted the child to look like…her eyes, eyebrows, and all her delicate features. When Liyuan was born, she was just as I had hoped and imagined. In China where each family is limited to one child, a child is indeed a treasure. It was no exception in my family.

The arrival of Liyuan made worldly life holy and rich.

I need not go into too much detail regarding the countless threads of love and emotion binding mother and child—that I believe any normal person can appreciate. That type of love is etched on one's bones and carved into one's heart. I was a loving and responsible mother, to the point that you can say that I doted on her. Oftentimes I found myself immersed in her every little smile and childish word. Even her sneezes caused me to have palpitations: I was afraid that she was going to be sick.

During Chinese New Year of 1991, I found that my daughter looked gaunt and had a poor appetite. She was in the second grade then. One day she said to me: "Mama, I'm very tired and my bones hurt..." At that moment I was in the kitchen cooking, and a dark thought flashed in my mind: "Oh, no, I am going to lose her..." Soon thereafter, she was diagnosed with leukemia.

Liyuan was admitted to Beijing Children's Hospital, and in the course of treatment, she endured severe suffering. I thought to myself, good or bad, let this be resolved soon. I could not bear to see her go through the unending injections, chemotherapy, transfusions, and marrow extractions.

After every session, Liyuan would try to shrug off her pain, saying: "Mother, it is pretty fun actually, it does not hurt at all now." Even her doctor praised her, with tears in his eyes, for being so courageous...(At this writing, I am once again racked by sobs. I cannot contain this strong feeling of motherly love. Forgive me for ending these recollections here.)

Three months later, my young daughter passed away under my caresses. Her final words to me were: "Mama, you will always be my wonderful Mama..." She was not even ten.

I was strangely calm at the moment of her passing, being sustained by an invisible power. As I left the hospital and looked up at the starry night sky, I tried to look for the star where I might belong. Was it also my time to leave this world. It must be so!

How did I live through the days after her passing? Many people may not grasp what I have to tell. In the beginning, I simply ate, slept and gained weight. From the outside, it did not seem I was going through a great ordeal at all. I worked hard to suppress my pain and imitate Grandma, trying to learn from and personally feel her attitude toward death. But imitation, in the end, is still not the real thing. Deep in my heart my pain grew more severe each day, until one day it simply erupted. I shut my doors and began to scream and cry. I thought that if I created a big enough commotion, I might rouse the high masters and guardians. Indeed, I needed some answers!

Guanyin Bodhisattva finally appeared and explained that this was meant to temper my heart and Liyuan's heart. She also revealed a vision of Liyuan's departure: she was escorted by a group of angels in white; while in her hand she held the hairpiece I had given her. (She had shed all her hair due to the chemotherapy. Prior to her cremation, I had cut my own hair and placed it on her head.) In the vision I saw her soul frolicking with the other angels, my hairpiece in hand, and not showing a sign of sadness.

That vision gave me some comfort. But when I turned to face my home, empty and devoid of life, with all of Liyuan's belongings laid out, my grief quickly returned. More and more I felt this means of "tempering" was too cruel. How could such cruelty be tempering when clearly it was destructive of life? I felt overwhelmed by regret.

Thinking back on my response to the holy patriarch who asked if I could make sacrifices, I felt myself the victim of an enormous trick. I was wrong to have made a vow of renunciation. Little had I known it would not be enough to renounce fame and fortune; I would also have to give up my only daughter.

At that moment such wishes as "enlightening all sentient beings" suddenly felt to me like empty absurdities. Like an avalanche in the high mountains, my faith collapsed utterly in a moment. When one's heart is consumed by rage, all communion with the heavens comes to a stop.

First of all I pulled down all my mandalas, and then I tore up some pictures of the Buddha. I stared into the quiet sky and resolved unbendingly to end my own life. "I will make sure all your plans for me will be in vain," I said to the heavens. After coming to this decision, I made preparations for the final step.

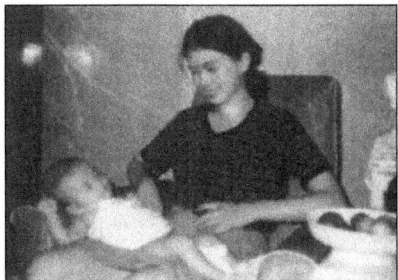

Yuan Liyuan was a lovely girl whom many people adored.

— 13 —

Suicidal Encounters

At first I chose the window in my office. The Central Television Building has twenty-four floors, and I was on the twenty-second. My attempt would surely be successful if I simply jumped from my own office window. On the way to the cafeteria I checked the spot where I would land, and found it to be full of pedestrians. This did not appeal to me—it would put people in a bad mood and make them feel disgust.

Next I bought sleeping pills, but did not know the pharmacy would only dispense six pills per prescription, so I had to store them over a period of time. Strangely enough, out of three prescriptions the pharmacist made a mistake on two and gave me vitamins instead.

I purchased a sharp knife, thinking to slash my wrists. Just as I was preparing to use it, the doorbell rang—my friends had come to visit. I did not want to risk being rescued and taken to the hospital, because then I would have to go on living.

Later, I decided on an ideal plan: on my next working trip away from Beijing, I would have an accident. This would show reasonable consideration for friends and relatives who cared about me. I chose the coastal city of Qingdao in Shandong Province, a place that offered suitable subjects for filming.

Qingdao is a beautiful ocean-side city with a rich heritage. My production crew and I were received by staff from the local television station, who briefed us on interview subjects and locations. I chose a very small island off the coast for our filming. The island had a small schoolhouse with only eight students in three different grades. What interested me were all the hidden reefs we had to pass on the way to the island, as well as the rough, perilous waves— that was what I had been waiting for. Since my mind was made up, our Qingdao Television colleagues could only agree to make arrangements, but first we had to wait for the tide.

Two days prior to our island excursion, as I anticipated my deliverance, I accepted a friend's suggestion to visit Laoshan. Laoshan is an important site for the Quanzhen sect of Chinese Taoism. Though not very familiar with Taoism, I had seen the peaceful composure of blue-robed Taoists with their hair in topknots.

Our route took us past a small food stall, and my friend urged me to sample some local specialties. I agreed and was just getting seated when the proprietor cried out in pleasant surprise: "Look quickly, Elder Zhang has come!" All I saw was an old man in a droopy hat, dressed in farmer's clothes with a rope belt coming down the rocky path.

Even my local guides became excited, for Elder Zhang was the most admired adept of Mount Lao, and many people came here from across the country specifically to visit him. But he did not relish meeting such visitors. His comings and goings were unpredictable, and he never dressed like a practicing Taoist. Instead, he wore the garb of a farmer the whole year long, with a straw hat to cover his face. Because the food hawker was a local, he immediately recognized Elder Zhang. He excitedly told us: "You are lucky to meet with him so quickly—there are many who stay here for months without being able to find him."

My guide quickly went to meet him as she was an admirer who wanted to ask his guidance on many matters. Elder Zhang spoke briefly with her, then turned to me and said, "You had best not go out to sea in the near future: there will be disaster on the water. You still have a long road ahead of you. Death will come to all of us sooner or later, so what is your hurry?"

After delivering this short message, he turned and walked off. My guide put much faith in the words of Elder Zhang, and upon returning to the Qingdao Television office she told her supervisor of this strange conversation. Out of consideration for my safety, the local crew then canceled our plans to visit the island. My vehement protests landed on deaf ears.

From Qingdao I proceeded to Mount Tai—another notable mountain in Shandong Province—and stayed at an inn on the mountain. On that day, a child accidentally fell from a nearby cliff which dampened the spirits of the locals and tourists. Not wanting to cast a worse shadow on the mood of people in this area, I temporarily suspended my suicide plans.

This particular inn was situated very close to the temple of Lady Tai, a goddess who was said to live among the ruby-fingered clouds of dawn. The proximity to Taoists, with their philosophy and technique of cultivation, proved to be a great lesson for me. Historically, Mount

Tai has long been the location where kings and emperors received their investiture. Many past emperors, upon taking the throne, would come to worship and seek favor from the Mount Tai deities. Because of the unique scenery and cultural context here, this region was among the first to be designated a key global heritage and conservation site by the United Nations.

I did receive some healing on Mount Tai. During my *dream yoga,* the Lady of Mount Tai[14] compounded a mixture of medicine for me. By her side was a boy-guardian who handed me the medicine with reluctance. Apparently he thought that someone like me was not worth bothering with.

Not far from Mount Tai is the city of Qufu—home of the sage Confucius. There I visited the Confucian temple and the Kong family burial ground called Kong Grove. In the Forest of Kong the illustrious and the revered were buried under rows of old tombstones among the deep grass. Outside the gates were signs hanging everywhere for the "Kong Estate Tavern." It all felt like clouds drifting before my eyes, like an illusion or dream.

The last thing I expected to encounter against the backdrop of ancient Chinese culture at Mount Tai and Qufu was the holy mother Mary. Thinking back now, during that whole trip I seemed to be heeding one summons after another from the beyond.

After my failed attempt at suicide in Qingdao, the latent spiritual energy at those Taoist and Confucian sites continued to work their effects on me. My pain was ameliorated, but I still felt downcast. I proceeded on my journey until I arrived at the nondescript little county seat of Pingyin. Pingyin was known for plentiful production

---

14 The Lady of Mount Tai is a Taoist goddess who is thought by some to be an emanation of Guanyin Bodhisattva.

of roses, with roses being grown on farms that stretched as far as the eye could see. I found a room at the county government guesthouse.

That night I experienced a remarkable dream: an unknown woman appeared before me, holy and dignified. Though dressed in simple garb, she showed an air of elegance and grace. People told me that this woman's son had died, but she endured her sorrow and was silently doing her utmost to benefit humankind. She had encountered one trial after another.

I woke from this sad, tearful dream feeling more depressed than before. I could not make out who this woman was, and what her association with me was. Early the next day, a friend took me to view the rose gardens. Around eleven in the morning, the weather turned gloomy, and a heavy rain began to fall. My friend said, "I'll take you where we can find shelter." In mysterious tones he added, "Don't ask, you'll find out when we get there."

We drove to a nearby village. After the rain stopped, we walked through the village to the foot of a mountain where one could see gothic-style structures. My friends told me that this was the Mount of the Holy Mother. There is a church on top of this mountain that had been built over one hundred years before by a Catholic priest from Austria. This mountain was close to Mount Tai and Qufu, and not far away the Yellow River flowed past. At that time, wild roses were in full bloom all over the mountain.

It was a steep hike up the stone steps to the mountaintop, and the path leading up was called the "Bitter Path." Along the Bitter Path one could see the story of Mary, from the birth of Jesus to his eventual crucifixion, told on a series of stone plaques. There were thirteen of these "bitter" scenes in all.

I hiked along this path, stopping to read the inscription on each plaque. When I read the last plaque, where Mary faced the loss of her son with serenity, I thought of my dream of the night before. Reaching the top, as I looked upon the picture of Christ's crucifixion, I cried.

I sat silently in the Church of the Holy Mother for three hours, facing this great mother from the West, and began to feel much more at peace. Simultaneously, I began to wonder. What are the differences in essence between Buddhists and Taoists in China and the Catholics and Protestants in the West? Do contradictions exist in the realm beyond the white clouds? Are there national boundaries? Are there doctrinal disputes? Why is there so much strife among human beings? Why is it that people have so many disputes of faith? Why do differing approaches to knowledge produce so much prejudice?

Instead of finding the quietude I had sought, I had even more unanswered questions than before.

Yuan Miao

Since my visit to Holy Mother Mountain in Pingyin County, Shandong Province, I have had feelings for this great mother figure of the West. This picture was taken at a church in New York.

— 14 —

Uniting with the Way of Heaven: Taking All Faiths as My Teachers

Putting aside an endless tangle of theoretical questions to face the deaths and separations that had befallen me, I began to reflect deeply. In reality I, like everyone else, am moving rapidly toward the moment of death without a moment's pause. The Taoist Elder Zhang had said, "There is no hurry." Our life-force grows weaker continually, and time passes moment by moment. Like a shape reflected on the surface of a lake, we can suddenly disappear without a trace. Just as shepherds herd sheep and cattle into a corral, disease and old age will eventually usher us to our deaths. No place on earth is free from death; certainly and unavoidably, death will one day find us. But because the time of death is uncertain, people habitually regard it as something far in the future. This attitude is a form of self-deception.

The reality of life is that sooner or later, we all encounter death and separation. It is the same for everyone. In the first ten years of life, we are only children. After the age of twenty, we are beset by increasing pain, worry, conflict, and sickness. Additionally, we spend a great deal of our time in sleep, and the fleeting pleasures we take are like knives caked with honey that eventually bring pain and suffering. So only by grounding one's heart in the impermanence of all things can we truly be free from meaningless afflictions caused by attachment.

Regardless of who we are, as death approaches we are utterly alone. At that moment, neither fame and wealth nor good friends and relatives can help us. Except for our spiritual qualities, nothing else is of any use at that moment. The only things that can help are the realizations and energies deposited in our subtle consciousness by self-cultivation. The imprint on our soul remaining from our proper conduct and proper thoughts is all that helps us at the moment of death. Thus, while we are alive, it is vital to cultivate our consciousness. And if we believe in some type of afterlife, then death is similar to changing one's clothes. You take off the old and then put on the new. It is that simple.

In facing the unfortunate events in our lives, we need to keep one perspective in mind—to mesh with life, to mesh with the Way of Heaven. If we are tested and tried by the heavens, there must be a good reason behind this. Since it is only a matter of time until death comes, why not step beyond the world's entanglements with an open, accepting heart and seek liberation from samsara[15] and its recurrent separations. Why not plunge into the expansive, compassionate arms of the universe, and fully embrace its truth?

---

15 Samsara is the birth-death cycle of reincarnation. Sentient beings follow one of the six paths of transmigration while experiencing this cycle (devas, asuras, humans, beasts, hungry ghosts, and hell-dwellers). For human beings, samsara is thus the cycle of reincarnation in the human world.

After a period of contemplation I felt new depth and expansiveness of spirit; I grew better at absorbing and accepting.

During my career as a director at Central Television, I worked on two interesting documentary series. One series was "Splendors of Cathay," and the other program, out of the international department, was "People and Nature." "Splendors of Cathay" gave me the opportunity to visit every province in China, and to explore to my heart's content the surviving traces from over five thousand years of Chinese history. I also had the privilege of seeing everyday life from the perspective of ordinary people, with all their expressions of happiness and grief. During the production of this program I also visited rare sites not accessible to most travelers. For instance, I went to the Han tomb complex where mummies in jade armor had been excavated. I went into a newly discovered 600,000-year-old cavern in which there were astonishing natural wonders.

Working in the international department on the series "People and Nature," I had the opportunity to travel in foreign countries. This gave me a chance to understand other cultures, particularly the religious culture of the West. Soaring Gothic arches and the tiled roofs of Eastern temples are equally attractive to me. I have always felt very close to the essential nature inherent in these buildings of different external styles. Although the "I" is contained in my own body, I know that Truth does not change shape due to linguistic or architectural expressions. It lies outside of any specific form.

Around the world we see the sun rise at different time intervals and experience its light. Whether at the North Pole or the equator, what people see is the same sun. Similarly, both Eastern and Western religions serve as a bridge to the Truth.

In a sense, what I went through gave me a calm appreciation of an eternal presence in the universe. I decided to be one with the heavenly Tao, to "follow nature," to do by *non-doing*.

Among those I am close to, not only are there Buddhist monks and Tibetan living buddhas, but also Taoist elders, Catholic fathers, Protestant pastors, and Islamic clerics. They have relayed the same message to me, albeit through different modes of realization: to love the ways of nature, have faith and govern oneself. Although they differ greatly in their rituals and methods of spiritual seeking, I get back to the source by going beyond the humanly determined variations, thus tasting for myself the peak of existence and reclaiming the radiant realm of *Pure Suchness*.[16] In the process I have reached a conclusion: it takes great perseverance to gain blessings through spiritual seeking, but this is not noble. A noble seeker is one for whom spiritual cultivation is not a refuge, but a form of service to others.

When interviewed by a Chinese radio station in Los Angeles, I was asked who my masters are. I responded that my first master was my Grandmother, and then came everyone who gave me guidance, whether intentionally or not. The masters in the heavens have expressed to me that my heart must be as broad as the ocean, and I should take all faiths, all dharmas, as my teachers. Even those who have hurt or insulted me have in one respect furthered my growth, and can be called my teachers.

Countless times I have told myself: since there is nowhere to run and hide, better to be more demanding on myself. If I am to seek, let me take the high road that connects me directly to the universal essence. It is not for me to waste my life-force going in circles at a

---

16 Pure Suchness (zhenru) is the state of unhindered spontaneity achieved by entering the pure ground of being.

middling level. On this harsh and demanding road of cultivation, I have kept my good conscience and spontaneity, and at the same have distilled my devotion and energy.

My samsaric ordeals of loss have given rise in my heart to another aspiration: I wish to remind people of the essential value of life, and the truth that death does not automatically release one from suffering. I must maintain a steady, persevering heart, and walk my life's journey courageously to the end.

— 15 —

Travelers in the Bardo Realm

What really happens after people die? Is it true that we are like lamps that simply burn out when we die? Certain personal experiences tell me that reincarnation is an undisputable reality. When our bodies die, our spirits enter a transition-state between one incarnation and the next. In the Tibetan tradition, this is called the Bardo realm.

What sort of experiences do "travelers" in the Bardo realm live through? What follows is my personal experience of three incidents, which may add to the reader's understanding.

First I will tell about my family friend, Uncle Zhang:

Uncle Zhang was an old friend of my parents. When he was fifty years old, he developed cirrhosis of the liver, and my mother gave him treatments. (While my grandfather was alive, he had been especially fond of my mother and had transmitted certain healing techniques to her.) The doctor found that Uncle Zhang's illness was already beyond help and would prove fatal within a year. With my mother's help, however, Uncle Zhang managed to live three more years.

During the last two months of his life, he and his wife expressed a wish that he could stay in our home for a while: "I'd like to tend the altar for you every day, Ma'am." Our family altar was small, but impressive nevertheless. After moving into our house, Uncle Zhang spent his days busying about the altar. I could see that his heart was filled with fear.

One day he came to my mother to make a confession: "Ten years ago when I was in a position of authority, I took advantage of my power to pocket a sum of public money. Will I go to hell after I die because of this?"

My mother told him that only if he were genuinely repentant, and if he built up merit to make up for his fault, he would be absolved of this karma. So Uncle Zhang anonymously donated a sum of money toward disaster relief. Shortly afterward, he was hospitalized due to his worsening condition.

One evening Mrs. Zhang phoned me, asking me to visit her husband in the hospital. "He would very much like to see you," she said. So I went to the hospital and sat next to his bed. By then he had been without solid food for three days, and was relying on intravenous feeding. He was very pleased to see me, and tried to sit up, saying: "I feel hungry, please Yuan Miao, feed me something." I took the porridge bowl from his wife's hand and began to feed him. After swallowing only two spoonfuls he suddenly felt a sharp pain, and beads of sweat stood out on his forehead. His wife sounded the emergency buzzer, and a nurse rushed to his side. He calmed down after she gave him an injection for the pain.

Returning home that night, I went to bed and fell asleep immediately. A dark and narrow passageway appeared in my dream.

After passing through this long corridor, an owl appeared before me; then I saw a group of strangers singing around a bonfire. Within the bonfire lay a coffin. I was roused from my dream by a call from Mrs. Zhang, informing us that her husband had passed away.

A week after Uncle Zhang's death, his bardo-body appeared before me in a tranquil guise. He said to me: "I'm here for a short visit this time, but next time I would like to put myself under your spiritual guidance."

My second story is about my housekeeper, Ms. Wei Yafang:

Wei Yafang was originally from Datian Village in Baiyang Marsh. She was a good-natured, intelligent girl, whom we called Little Fang. Little Fang had an intriguing karmic relationship to my family, and it all began with a documentary film.

Back in 1988, I led a production crew to Hebei Province to shoot a program tided "Life in Baiyang Marsh." To make our portrayal authentic, we stayed in a village called Wang's Stockade, located on an island in the marsh. We settled in and informed local officials we were there to capture the genuine local lifestyle and culture of these wetland villages. We were not only interested in daily life, but in customs surrounding childbirth, marriage and water burials. The unique marshland environment had given rise to characteristic folkways, and many such folkways could be seen in their child rearing, weddings, and traditional water burial customs. We quickly completed most aspects of our filming, except the water burial part, because we did not know when someone was going to die.

The ranking official in the county seat made our needs known to lower officials throughout the area. Everyone was asked to be on the lookout for someone near death so the film crew could make the necessary preparations. Quickly, news reached our crew that an octogenarian in a nearby village was in the terminal stage of cancer, and doctors gave him only a few days to live. His village was only forty minutes by rowboat from where we stayed.

Over the next several days, we used the telephone in Wang's Stockade to ask for news from the sick man's village, and meanwhile we finished all other footage for the film. The only outstanding segment that remained was the water burial. My crew and I began to grow restless. Conditions in the marshland village were beginning to take their toll on us, and what was more, we did not know when our wait would be over.

One humdrum afternoon, I organized a meeting of our film crew at the village guesthouse, where male members of our crew were staying. This so-called *guesthouse* was merely a quadrangle of rooms around a courtyard, surrounded by farm shacks. As I walked in with the engineer, we noticed an old gentleman of the neighborhood sitting on a rock near the door, enjoying the sun with his walking stick in hand.

As soon as I walked in, the male crew members began to complain that they could not take it any more. No one in the crew wanted to stay. As a director, I had to weigh the importance of the water burial footage against our failing morale. I announced to everyone: "Be patient for another three days, and if nothing happens we will leave."

Our meeting lasted for about thirty minutes, and afterwards I returned with the engineer to the women's quarters in a farmer's house ten minutes away by foot. As we exited, the elderly gentleman was still sitting on the rock, clearly relaxed and enjoying himself.

About an hour later, a barrage of thunder and lightning struck the village. Great gusts of wind blew woven-reed panels all over the village. After this storm, as the villagers rushed about cleaning up the mess, the landlady's granddaughter came running breathlessly to tell us that Wei Jicai, the former mayor, had died of a heart attack during the lightning storm. Mr. Wei had been that elderly gentleman who had been sitting outside our meeting place only a moment ago!

Our entire crew was rather shocked at this news. The men had seen the old man sitting at their doorway every day. They had no idea who he was, just that he lived in the neighborhood. The current mayor told us that Mr. Wei had done many good things for the village, earning the admiration of the villagers.

Our landlady told us that many villagers were now making negative remarks, saying that the television people had put a jinx on Mr. Wei Jicai. They said that the *lady director,* in particular, had insisted on filming a water burial, and had openly been waiting for someone to die. This had the effect of putting a jinx on the former mayor.

I contacted the county supervisor that very night to ensure that a proper funeral was to be provided for the elderly Mr. Wei.

The supervisor obligingly gave instructions to utilize a coffin that had been locked away for years, [17]along with musical instruments and funeral trappings from the late Ch'ing dynasty. The next day, when all the long-prohibited funeral accoutrements were hauled to Wang's Stockade, a new rumor started circulating among the villagers: the former mayor was being repaid for his good karma. He had suffered from heart disease all these years, but he happened to die right while they were making a film. How many people have a chance to go out in style like that?

---

17 Because the Chinese government advocated the adoption of modern customs, many folk customs were prohibited.

Inwardly I addressed the old man: "Dear Mr. Wei, you have done good things for people in your community, and you have won their respect. Your life has been meaningful. Please do not be overly attached to the human world. Even though you departed suddenly, please do not be sad. Go ahead to the heavenly realm."

On the third night, after we completed filming an elaborate water burial, I saw an image of Mr. Wei's bardo body fly from the roof of his house into the sky.

Four years after this happened, I no longer remembered Mr. Wei Jicai. One early morning as I lay between sleep and waking, I saw many flower wreaths. I was walking alongside a young man dressed in white, escorting him between rows of wreaths to a bridge. He turned to me, told me not to send him further, and then crossed over the bridge himself. Before long he returned, holding the hand of a young woman. He said he was grateful to me, and was giving this young woman to me.

Later, I told my husband this dream story, and he thought it was quite interesting.

That afternoon as I sat in the office preparing for a trip to Sweden, the security officer at the doorway rang for me. I was told that a colleague had found a housekeeper for me. She had come from Baiyang Marsh, and was waiting at the building entrance to meet me. This was a bit sudden for me, as I was preparing to go to Sweden. Although a suitable housekeeper was difficult to find, I had planned to wait until after my trip. My friend told me that this was the girl's first time in Beijing, and I should at least show her around a bit before sending her back.

I walked to the entrance of the building and found a shy country girl waiting there for me. Seeing me she said, "I know you. My great-uncle's name was Wei Jicai. My mother and I were at Great Uncle's funeral, and we saw you in a big straw hat, directing the television crew." I said to her then and there: "You don't have to go back." To this day my housekeeper Wei Yafang still lives in my Beijing house, though she has found other work by now.

This last account is about a woman whom I never met face-to-face:

It was in spring of 1998 when I was preparing to make yet another working trip to Xiamen. I went to bed early that night because I had to catch an early flight the next morning. In my dream I saw a woman I did not recognize being dragged into a car. Then I saw the malevolent face of a murderer, and the cruel look in his eyes as he pushed the woman out of the car. This made me break out in a cold sweat, and after that I saw a tall, thin man approaching me with his child. He told me they were afraid to go home, because the minute they stepped through the door they felt chills. The next moment I found myself in their home, and saw the child's teddy bear moving. I asked the bear who it was, and the bear identified itself as the child's mother. I asked her why she was there, and she replied "I cannot leave my child. This teddy bear was my child's favorite toy, and he used to hug it constantly."

I told her that remaining there was not good for her child or her husband, and she ought to leave quickly. The teddy bear responded, "I don't know where to go. I don't know the way." I told her to look for Guanyin Bodhisattva, and I promised to help her find the way.

Later, on the way to the airport, I told my husband of this dream. He seemed concerned for my safety, and asked me to call him when I arrived in Xiamen.

But on arriving in Xiamen I immediately got involved with work, and did not have time to call until late that evening. My husband's shaken voice on the line told me what had happened after he dropped me off at the airport. "I went over to my mother's home for a visit, and from there I phoned a childhood friend named Jingjing. He is a sports reporter for Beijing Television. Jingjing told me that his wife was murdered not long ago. She was forced into a car at gunpoint, and later the body was thrown into a river..." At this point my husband's voice started to quiver. "It was like the dream you told me, down to the last detail. I'm really afraid. What should we do? Jingjing tried to take his child back home, but the minute they stepped in the door, the child started crying..."

I instructed my husband to pray for Guanyin at our private altar, seeking a peaceful passage for the soul of the murdered woman. After this occurrence I asked my unseen master why bardo beings I didn't recognize were coming before me? The response I received was that all this was happening to train my bodhi-mind.

There have been other occurrences like this, including the bardo body of a certain county supervisor who begged me to smooth his wife's mortal passage. There was also the bardo body of a woman who asked me to take care of her daughter. I discovered that there are longtime travelers in the bardo realm, and there are new travelers also. The longtime travelers parted from worldly existence years ago, and the new ones have recently left it. For the most part, these bardo bodies are in a restless, lonely state. The longtime ones are in the worst condition due to their long fruitless search for a final destination, and they may begin causing trouble and harassing the living.

These occurrences are what people traditionally have called

haunting. There are two types of people who need not go through this bardo state because the strength of their positive or negative karma is such that it immediately dictates a certain destination. The first type, through good deeds and striving during their lifetimes, have tempered their souls so that power of thought will take them directly to higher planes of incarnation. The latter type, who have led evil, degraded lives, will quickly descend into one of the lower planes. Additionally, death for someone who has attained the Tao is an extraordinarily beautiful and triumphant moment. Heavenly devas,[18] buddhas, and your unseen root master will come to meet you, just as your relatives would welcome you back from years of wandering in foreign lands.

I don't want to go into any more detail on my impressions of the bardo realm, to prevent being misidentified as a "channel" or psychic. I am not cut out to be a psychic, but personal experiences have led me to a certain understanding. Human life in its physical phase is like an island in the ocean: only a small part appears above the surface, while the deeper, more genuine part remains submerged. Where do we come from? Where are we going? This double question is easy for people to ignore. People often focus upon transitory instances in the zone between, with no chance to explore life's truest wellspring.

As I write this, I feel sorry for travelers who remain adrift in the bardo realm; I hope they will not forget the bitterness they have suffered. Once they reincarnate as human beings, let them exert themselves in self-cultivation and aspire to ultimate liberation. Also, I hope that those among the living will cherish their lives and use their life-energy properly. Let them reach understanding of death as it is,

---

[18] Devas are beings that occupy heavenly realms in the Buddhist cosmology. They are similar to Western angels or deities.

so they fear neither living nor dying. Let them unlock their spiritual wisdom, using transient life to explore the infinite.

In the *Tibetan Book of the Dead* we can find in-depth teachings on the true condition of the bardo body and its modes of liberation. Here I have touched only superficially on this subject.

There are three beautiful ways to die: dying without regret, dying without fear, and dying joyfully. After all, death is not really an end; it marks the beginning of a whole new "life!"

— 16 —

A Glorious Procession of Rinpoches

Perhaps because I have some Tibetan blood, I have always felt specially attracted to the Tibetan plateau. There are those who label Tibetans as being backward and ignorant of modern technology, and therefore reject their ways completely. I, on the other hand, believe that their pristine setting on a high-altitude plateau, combined with the honest, peaceful customs that have emerged there, have furthered the spiritual accomplishments of many seekers. Many of these seekers have been renunciates who in Tibet are given the title Rinpoche, which means "precious one."

Due to the loosening of restrictive religious policies following the Cultural Revolution, I found chances to make contact with Tibetan Rinpoches. The first time was in the summer of 1986. That summer, I took my daughter and mother to Wutai Mountain in Shanxi Province. Wutai Mountain is not only one of the "four sacred mountains" of

Chinese Buddhism, it is a restful, refreshing spot known as a "wonderland of coolness" even in the heat of summer.

Wutai has been long known as the sacred place of Manjusri Bodhisattva. In the Tibetan tradition, Manjusri is the great root master who is said to belong in the same spirit-lineage as the great heavenly master Padmasambhava.[19] When my mother was pregnant with me, it was Manjusri Bodhisattva who appeared before Grandma and gave me my name, Yuan Miao. Thus, everything about Wutai Mountain seems to hold special significance for me.

The Hall of Ten Directions is the most orthodox Vajrayana monastery at Wutai Mountain. In addition to hosting and sponsoring various Tibetan Buddhist ceremonies, this monastery also serves as a reception place for many Tibetan pilgrims. After we arrived in the Hall of Ten Directions, a young monk named Danchue-jenzan guided us to the shrine-hall at the rear. After performing a ritual we walked out of the monastery, and noticed that Danchue-jenzan was following. Blushing and speaking in broken Chinese, he said that his guardian spirit had revealed in a dream that an older sister would visit the temple that day. He sensed I was the sister of last night's dream, so he was overjoyed when I addressed him as 'Younger Brother."

The day after that, Danchue-jenzan came to our room and informed us that a great rinpoche would perform a tantric initiation at the Hall of Ten Directions for head monks from surrounding temples. In fact, this was to be the first time since the relaxing of religious policies that Wutai would host a tantric initiation ceremony. Because of limited space, attendance was restricted to leading members of local temples. Being an assistant to the abbot of the host temple, he

---

19 Padmasambhava was a Vajrayana master who left India to teach Buddhism in Tibet in the middle of the Seventh Century. He is the first patriarch of the Nyngma School.

could arrange for my participation, and he wanted to know if I was interested in attending. I agreed to this special opportunity, and had the privilege of receiving an anointment from Gadeng Rinpoche of the Lablung Monastery. From this point on, more and more rinpoches have become part of my spiritual life.

I am very fortunate that through careful selection, I have been able to meet and form ties with many excellent and advanced rinpoches. Among these rinpoches, I have a deep connection to Gangje Rinpoche who makes his home in Italy. During his brief and busy stay in Beijing, he took time to teach me his set of tantric Buddhist calisthenics. His mudras are like his appearance, filled with inclusiveness and spiritual force. And then there is Uncle Rinpoche, Duoshi-Losangtu-Danch'iongpai, who wrote *Love: An Eruption of Heart-Wisdom,* with whom I also share a special karmic relationship. Three days after my arrival in America, I arranged through friends to invite him to America. His lecture at the University of California left a deep impression on many people.

Uncle Rinpoche is professor of Tibetan language at the Gansu Province Nationalities Institute. He is a learned scholar, and his command of Chinese is unequalled by any other rinpoche. Because of this, he is uniquely qualified to instruct and edify Chinese-speaking people. Both Uncle Rinpoche and Gangjia Rinpoche are members of the Geluk sect of Tibetan Buddhism. The Geluk School is known for its commitment to Buddhist philosophy. It stresses systematic theoretical studies and the integration of doctrine with practice.

The rinpoches of the Nyngma sect, because they wear red-colored hats, are also known as the red-hat lamas. Jarang-Longje Rinpoche has not worn "worldly clothes" since taking up a monastic life at age five. Even during the height of the Cultural Revolution, when he was forcibly ejected from his temple to become a cowherd, he covered his body with a single red cloth. When he came to Beijing and stayed with me, I recommended that he purchase a red warm-up suit to avoid troublesome attention from people unfamiliar with his tradition. He was very easygoing, and wore this red casual suit during his visit. During that period he transmitted to me a text that he himself had uncovered. He expounded the *Tibetan Book of the Dead,* and taught me specific methods for liberating the bardo body after death.

Another Nyngma Rinpoche, Azuo Bala, is tall and imposing in build. In Tibet he is believed to be an incarnation of Padmasambhava. Even his features remind me of Padmasambhava's wrathful form—Daweide Vajra.[20]

Azuo Bala has a portable temple because he gives teachings in many places and is often away from Lhasa. He sometimes takes over a thousand monks along with him to the sky burial fields, where he guides them in learning *powa* practices. Such practices are conducted deep in the Tibetan interior away from tourists. *Powa* techniques use *dhyana* meditation[21] and sympathetic resonance to assist the dying and to prepare oneself for the afterlife. It is an ancient form of spiritual practice in which aspirants turn prayer wheels and chant mantras. Drawing on power imparted by Azuo Bala, they allow their consciousness to come and go freely through the crown chakra, so that when they eventually enter a bardo state, they can navigate easily

---

20 When first teaching Buddhism in Tibet, in order to subjugate demons by tantric means, Padmasambhava appeared in a ferocious form with bull's head called Daweide Vajra.

21 Dhyana meditation is a practice of progressively deeper concentration states taught in many schools of Buddhism. The Chinese word "Chan" (Japanese: Zen), as in the "Chan School," is a transliteration of dhjana.

to their final destination. At the same time, this practice helps lessen their attachment and greed. When the right conditions are met, the successful practitioner will feel an itch or pain on top of the head, accompanied by swelling or softening. For some, a small crack will appear on the head and blood will trickle out. The teacher will then insert a small blade of grass to confirm this attainment.

Azuo Bala speaks with gravity and does not smile lightly, so some people are afraid of him. He can stare at someone without flinching for more than twenty minutes, until the other person breaks out into a sweat. He will not let up until he succeeds in shaking up the person's mental obstacles. His mental powers are strong because of his aspiration to help all beings toward enlightenment. Azuo Bala is also known as the "Rainbow Rinpoche," because wherever he appears a rainbow seems to follow. In his solemn moods he looks like a ferocious deity, but he also has a childlike side. One time he laughingly pulled on my two ears, saying that he would make them grow bigger. I then proceeded to pull on his ears to make them bigger as well. His little lama attendant was shocked to see my actions: strict etiquette would only permit me to join my hands and thank him for his blessing.

There is a step in *Yoga of Joy* called: "Oasis in the Desert," which combines a Tibetan prostration with movements that emerged from my inner nature. Azuo Bala thinks this posture is good not just for balancing energy circulation and hormone secretions, it also adjusts two modern-day diseases of the spirit: arrogance and karmic obstacles.

The name that Azuo Bala gave me is "Honche Tsuomu," which means Ocean of Bodhi.[22] A short blessing was often on his lips: *Hon-*

---
22 Bodhi means 'awakening.' To bring forth the bodhi-mind means resolving to be enlightened. In Mahayana Buddhism, bringing forth the bodhi-mind includes the resolve to enlighten all sentient beings.

che Tsuomu, zashe da-re! Zashe da-re means "bliss and fulfillment."

A total of over ten rinpoches have given me personalized instruction and dharma-transmissions. I have also learned from certain rinpoches without ever meeting them face-to-face. For instance, there was Hangen Lamajo Rinpoche from the Jixiang Scripture Institute in Seda County, Sichuan. Though he had already passed away when I spoke to his wife on the phone, his book *Sweet Beads of Dew* has been a great source of strength for me. Aside from that, I have felt his spirit-consciousness resonate with mine on many occasions.

Although I lived physically in Beijing, often I found that spiritually I was living among a glorious procession of rinpoches. The great self-mastery of the special ones, with their liberation in body, mind and speech, will always serve to rouse us and give us spiritual joy.

After coming to America, many people have asked me about the tantric practice of "dual cultivation," wanting to know if I followed this practice. My answer is yes, but this cannot be reduced to sexual union as some people might suppose. It is the dual cultivation of compassion and wisdom. I have in my possession some special tankas painted at Lablung Temple. One of them depicts two embracing Vajrasattva figures. I often tell people that in this picture, "the male figure represents compassion and the female represents wisdom. Joined together they are truth; they are the bodhi-mind after liberation." I fear that people will get a wrong or twisted idea about "dual cultivation."

As I think about this, the pure lucid eyes of many rinpoches appear before me. I realize it is difficult for ordinary people to appreciate holy and pure teachings from the snowy ranges of Tibet. In American bookstores I seldom see books which explain this satisfactorily. Here

I will quote a passage from the book *Love: An Eruption of Heart-Wisdom* by Losang Rinpoche. This should help the reader understand what "dual cultivation" means in Tibetan tantricism.

> *The Buddha of Bliss is a specific Buddha, not a general term for paired buddha figures. The Sanskrit word for Buddha of Bliss is Pramodya Buddha. At the Lablung Monastery, there is a special Pramodya Seminary devoted to practices related to this Buddha. Tantric yoga works of the Vajrayana Canon contain pictures of embracing male and female figures. As we remarked earlier, the Buddha image in Buddhism is an artistic form which holds symbolic meaning. Like the symbolic images of modern art, it cannot be understood in terms of visual form alone. However, the symbolic content in Buddhism fits a well-defined pattern, rather than being impressionistic. Detailed expositions of this can be found in the Supplementary Canon. Those who view Buddhism as superstitious "idol worship" are victims of a serious misunderstanding.*
>
> *Tibetan Buddhism uses the idea of yin-yang polarity to express the relation of matter and spirit, space and objects, substance and phenomena, action and knowing, bodily fluids and qi, manifest and unmanifest, etc. The two opposed sides presuppose each other; they are interdependent and inseparable. Such an inter-reliant relationship is called complementarity*

or "vajra nature." Complementarity allows life and the cosmos to remain in a state of vital homeostasis. When the balance is lost, or when yin and yang separate, the result will surely be decline and oblivion. Tantra is a method of cultivation which harmonizes yin-yang and releases latent potentials to elevate the life force. Images of buddhas embracing represent complementary relations within the human body, such as blood with qi. With respect to the noble path, the images signify pairs such as compassion and wisdom; with respect to achieved buddhahood, they signify relationships such as between the Buddha's substance with the Buddha's wisdom. All of these are interdependent pairs, with the male image representing the yang pole, and the female the yin pole. For example, in the dual image of the Pranidhi Vajras, the blue Buddha-father represents qi, and the red Buddha-mother represents blood. They are locked in an embrace, representing the interplay of blood and qi. Another example is the picture of Kalacakra Deities, in which the sky-blue Buddha-father represents the non-physical heaven-energy of empty space, while the ocher Buddha-mother stands for physical, earthly energy. Yellow and ocher are symbolic colors for earth. The two figures embrace to represent the interdependence of form and emptiness, or the union of space and energy. In most images of embracing buddhas, the male stands for compassion and is called the

Buddha-father, while the female stands for wisdom and is called the Buddha-mother. Compassion and wisdom are the two pillars of Buddha-dharma, and embracing figures symbolize the union of these two doctrines.

This has nothing to do with sensuality or animalistic lust. The highest tantric attainment is called "wisdom of blissful emptiness." Here "bliss" refers to a state experienced when *qi* moves freely through the central channel "Emptiness wisdom" is the intuition of emptiness gained while in this blissful state. No other meaning is intended."

Similarly, the nine steps of *Yoga of Joy* introduced in this book integrate the physical with the spiritual, the circulation of blood and subtle energy, and the principles of balance between Yin and Yang.

As I finish writing this chapter, I hope with sincere devotion to build a bridge between my readers and all those wonderful rinpoches. Simply put, may all sentient beings find "bliss and fulfillment... *Zashe da-re"*

– 17 –

Leave Everything and Go to America!

As early as July of 1985, Grandma told me that someday I would go to America. At the time I was excited and curious about such an opportunity; I wanted her to let me go right away, not wait for an indefinite future. Grandma told me: "That is a place of worldly dazzlements. Going now would not be good for your character." She repeatedly admonished me that prior to leaving, I must not reveal my attainments or tell secrets regarding my trip. Thus, the fact that someone from Beijing is now transmitting something called *"Yoga of Joy"* comes as a surprise to many people. That I can understand, because the proper conditions were not ready. It would have gone against my master's instructions to disclose prematurely why I was going to America.

I own a few condominiums in Beijing; three of them in the suburb of Changping. Changping is an area of splendid landscapes near the

Ming tombs and the Great Wall. I chose it because its distance from hectic city life makes it an ideal setting for secluded spiritual practice.

My husband was also a director with CCTV. He was handsome, fit, and upright in character—an outstanding man in all respects. I have already introduced another member of our family, our young housekeeper Little Fang. In addition, we were providing foster care for a child from the Beijing Orphans' Home. After coming to America, I received comforting news that this child has found a permanent home with an American couple.

For many years I obediently heeded my master's request and committed myself to silence. My friends and family simply thought I was hard to fathom in some ways, but no one could put their finger on the reasons why.

On the first day of the Chinese New Year, 1999, the Buddha-Mother appeared before me, instructing me to "leave everything behind and go to America!"

Although I had visited many countries, I had never been to America. My travel plans for 1999 had already been made, and America was not among them. Especially perplexing was my lack of friends or family in America. Even if I did come, what would I do there?

A few days later, my cousin introduced to me a Chinese-American woman from Silicon Valley in California. Her name was Chiling, and she lived in Beijing with her husband, doing business in computers. The moment Chiling and I met we felt like old friends. After living in Beijing for a year, Chiling sensed a stronger karmic tie with me than with anyone she had met in China. So Chiling and I got together several times. A month after we met she invited me to visit America with her, and I agreed. I immediately began applying for a personal passport.

In mid-May, American planes bombed the Chinese embassy in Yugoslavia, causing crowds of Beijing citizens to protest at the American embassy. Meanwhile, CCTV issued a directive canceling all trips to America for news coverage and program development. Right around that time, the Falungong Sect had some very visible clashes with the Chinese government, and tension was felt at every level nationwide. Anyone familiar with Chinese affairs knows this was an extremely difficult time for a Chinese citizen to receive an American visa. For one thing, CCTV, as the official mouthpiece of the Chinese government, restricted the activities of its journalists, and directors. Luckily, I gave people an impression of peace and calm, and my application for vacation time was smoothly approved. Things were tense at the American embassy, due to popular resentment stirred by the Belgrade bombing incident, and visa applications were routinely rejected, particularly for journalists making trips to America.

In July, when Rinpoche Gesang-rejie came to visit from Wutai Mountain, I asked him whether I would be visiting America. In answer he made a mudra and said, "It is in keeping with Buddha-dharma. May your wish be fulfilled."

The following day, July 12, I received a visa to travel to America after a two-minute interview. All that remained was to wait for Chiling to juggle her busy schedule a bit. Finally we settled on August 8 as my travel date.

I arrived in Silicon Valley on August 8 according to plan. On August 29, Chiling took me to tour a film studio in Hollywood. I recalled that a friend had introduced me to a contact in Los Angeles, so I made a phone call. Two hours prior to my departure, I had a brief meeting with this person, and we discussed the possibility of working on a worthwhile documentary project together.

My conversations with this person continued by phone after I returned to Beijing. In October this friend came to Beijing on business, and we had a second meeting. At that time, he thought that a person with my talents would make an ideal collaborator. He left Beijing after a ten-day stay, then invited me to work with him in America. Though there was a strong worldly flavor to this beginning, it was only through such worldly considerations that a "higher intention" could begin to operate in a tangible context.

Because I had made this specific contact, there was someone to receive me during my early days in America. This was a vital juncture that got things rolling. When the way is being paved for a dharma-path, the Buddha works with chains of circumstance that are beyond ordinary understanding. The transmission of Yoga of Joy could never have gotten this far without gracious, unrecognized acts on the part of many well-meaning people.

On midnight of November 11, Guanyin Bodhisattva appeared and urged me again to "Leave everything and go to America." This time she indicated a specific time and mode of departure. Only four days later, on November 15th, I left behind career and family, and headed for Los Angeles. On that very day, a prime time slot featured my newly completed environmental documentary, *Return of the White Egret,* while I was flying out of China!

Here I have written at some length about the details of my coming to America, because my countless viewers, friends and family have been in the dark about my departure from China. I want them to know the truth, and that I love them all very much.

— 18 —

I Shall Guide and Protect You

Letting go is an important practice for self-cultivation. The idea is simple, but hard to practice. There is a saying: "Small sacrifice, small gain; great sacrifice, great gain; no sacrifice, no gain." In the words of the Chan saying, "Be done with cliff-hanging and accept the consequences; once you have revived you will no longer be tricked by oblivion." Only in this way can a new life emerge.

Did my "new life" emerge in the turbulence of a trans-Pacific flight? It was not so easy! Even the famed characters in the Chinese classic novel *Journey to the West*,[23] on their way to bring holy Buddhist sutras back to China, had to encounter 81 different trials and tribulations. In the end Guanyin gave them a wordless book, and would not spare them their last trial—to watch their own bodies floating down the river.

When my departing flight landed in Shanghai, my emotions were

---

23 Journey to the West (Xiyouji) is a classical Chinese novel narrating the journey of Xuanzhuang and his disciples, who traveled from China to India in search of Buddhist scriptures. Though based on a historical journey, the novel is a mostly a work of fantasy.

in tumult as I waited for exit formalities. I used my portable phone to call my friends and family, to give my best wishes to every person who loved and cared for me. As the plane took off for America, I could not control my tears, being torn by feelings of reluctance and sentimental attachment.

At the time of my departure, my husband was in Macau preparing television coverage of that city's hand-over to China. Prior to his trip, I had revealed that it was time for me to go to America. He had listened disapprovingly, thinking that I was just babbling. When I really did leave, he was angry, and he decided to part ways with me.

My dear husband, my illustrious career, and a comfortable lifestyle were gone all in a flash. Even sunny Los Angeles welcomed me with a gloomy haze.

This is not to deny that the person who received me was a well-meaning advisor. He arranged for me to live in a beautiful new house, and entertained me with every courtesy. To this day I am thankful for such kindness.

But I found out quickly that even in this place of abundant sunlight, the darkness and prejudice of human hearts are no different than anywhere else. My forthright nature and guru-yogic state puzzled some people. They simply could not believe that a different kind of life was possible—it was something they had never been exposed to.

At that time, I began to realize that not only had I forsaken my home, career and marriage, I had also lost the supportive setting I had completely taken for granted at home. I had lived in an environment, up until that point, where I was trusted and treated with dignity. But since coming to America, amidst an ocean of dollars, credit cards, lotteries, and slot machines, my "empty nature" proved to be disappointing to certain people. Some even doubted my integrity and "usefulness."

The cold reality of my new surroundings, coupled with the loss of what I cherished, filled me with a sense of being sadly misunderstood. That was another period when earthly emotions severed my connection with wisdom and the Truth. Facing this strange and "cruel" world, I called out more than once from the depths of my heart: "My heavenly masters, my precious Guanyin, what shall I do?" During my lowest period, I packed up my things and went to the ocean. Perhaps the broad Pacific Ocean could deliver me from adversity.

On a sunny afternoon, the voice of Guanyin sounded from the deep beyond: "I shall guide and protect your journey!" My heart grew quiet, and I no longer felt wronged or humiliated. A hundred feelings welled up in my heart, and I could not keep from weeping. Over the next few days Los Angeles was filled with rain and thunder. My tears came down with the pouring rain to wash all the built-up ignorance and sorrow from my heart. For seven days, eating very little except some water and fruit, I wept, sometimes even without a particular reason or cause, just feeling touched by boundless pity and concern, for myself and for others. The more I cried, the lighter I felt; the more the tears flowed, the fewer obstacles I felt, until my heart was gradually at peace. In a deep meditative state, I discovered that my heart and throat chakras had opened completely! In that deep state of quietude my *fan-yin* (mantric voice) surfaced.

Many people who have experienced my mantric voice express surprise at the energy and beauty of these ethereal sounds. They do not see how sound waves produced by the human throat can have such effects on our heart and spirit. What is the secret behind this?

I will go into this question later when I introduce the *Nine Steps of Yoga of Joy*.

Now I will tell about "Stagnation" giving way to "Harmony."[24] With help from the expedient actions of my friends, I moved out of that fine new house and into a small, dingy room in San Gabriel. It was the smallest and simplest home I had ever lived in, but poverty was a lesson I had to learn as a precondition for my freedom and self-completion.

"Confront death and live anew"—this little room afforded my spirit a place to expand and fully manifest my nature. During my six months of residence there, from April to October 2000, my Yoga of Joy matured into a nine-step regimen suitable for transmission. As the saying goes: "Brown earth cannot cover a shining pearl." Many people of affinity heard about me and found their way to this little house, to seek the path of deliverance and learn Yoga of Joy. Soon the parking spaces near that humble house were hardly enough to accommodate my visitors. The eagerness of these truth-seekers afforded me joy and consolation.

In January of 2001, I was invited to lecture in Los Angeles at the Philosophical Research Society. One of the topics I spoke on, "Days Nearest to God," was my reflection on this amazing six months of my life.

Another bit of good news quickly followed—my residency status in America was approved. In the matter of a worldly dwelling place, I could dispense with my worries over the future.

---

24 "Stagnation" is a hexagram in the *I Ching*, symbolizing a situation in which Heaven does not interact with earth. The "Harmony" hexagram reverses this to express interplay between Heaven and earth, or yin and yang. To say 'Stagnation' gives way to 'Harmony' is like saying that the darkest time is before the dawn.

On the Wings of Phoenix Rising

Many well-meaning advisors came to me in response to karmic conditions, volunteering their help and ideas for developing Yoga of Joy. Their earnest aspiration and concern have renewed my faith and elevated the Dharma-nature.

As I write this in Malibu Beach facing the Pacific, the setting sun has turned the ocean surface into a golden expanse. On the other side of the Pacific, the sun is just rising over my motherland. To that place belongs the years gone by, with the imprint of my steps on a spiritual journey that continues to this day. It has been over fifteen years since Grandma's prophecy that I would one day come to America. Fifteen years of samsara, fifteen years of stumbling and getting up again. With an ordinary mind and body, I have come through life's extremities, and in the process I have obtained an enduring spiritual work. The travail of such a journey was enough to shake the heavens and wring tears from the eyes of gods, but I have come, from East to West to raise a "Joyful" banner. I have come to illuminate the meaning of life.

Though my temperament is still subject to many moods and feelings, I am no longer the old me. My "feelings" are now compassionate feelings that emerge from the emptiness of *prajna,* and their energy comes from the universal essence. Their source is the highest level of existence, coming from the guidance and protection of the Great Compassionate Guanyin!

— 19 —

Who Is the Shining One?

I used to be willing to try anything. Grandma once taught me a mudra and mantra for use in times of danger. On one occasion when I was riding on a crowded train, it was so crowded I could not find a place to sit. Believing that this constituted a bona-fide emergency (I could not work properly if I stood for the entire three-hour trip), I began to contemplate using my mudra and mantra to secure myself a seat. I rationalized to myself that as a special child of God, I should be afforded a seat. Standing is something reserved for the godless, not the saintly! I discovered a perfect target for my spell in a young man late in his teens. He pretended not to notice that a woman was standing while he sat comfortably. Thinking to myself that this young man was poorly raised and rude, I began to train my emergency mudra and mantra on him to make him give up his seat. After half an hour of effort, the young man still did not get up. In fact he relaxed even more, fell asleep, and eventually began to snore. He even stretched his legs further, pushing me toward the crowd!

Although this happened many years ago, I remember this lesson. There are many reasons why our intended mental powers lose effect. That day on the train I had violated a very simple rule, to be compassionate. I paid no heed to the karmic responsibility of engaging in such prohibited acts, and in the process had cheapened the idea of using mental powers.

There are many people in China who are blessed with extraordinary powers. I had the opportunity to meet the famed Zhang Baosheng and Xiong Zaiding. During a meal at the Beijing Hotel, I once witnessed Zhang use telekinetic force to slide all the silverware on our table into a heap. But once when I misplaced my CCTV identification badge and asked him to make it reappear, he responded that I was better off applying for a new one. Xiong Zaiding is a woman who lives in Hubei Province. After being cured of a strange disease by an "Old Man Without a Name," she did not eat solid food for eighteen years, yet remained very healthy and vibrant. Prior to coming to America, I heard she had become a mother.

I was once very fascinated with such "supernatural" occurrences and powers. But I was quickly reminded that such skills are not to be sought or displayed. It is better to be without them if they are not enlightening. The correct attitude is to sow without regard for the harvest, to cultivate without greed for returns. The cultivation of one's spirit is a very serious matter. There are different levels of attainment, and supernatural powers do not necessarily reflect a mature level. They are perhaps an expedient means, offered along the path, and their final purpose is to reach a vast and more open space. Without the perspective of *prajna*,[25] worldly

---

25 Prajna is non-dualistic wisdom which sees phenomenal form and underlying empty-naturedness as a unity. Prajna is treated at length in the Vajra Sutra and the Prajnaparamita Sutra. It is a key idea in the Madhyamika (Middle View) School.

psychic powers may lead people astray from the right path.

A physicist friend of mine had a series of paranormal reactions after receiving empowerment from a spiritual teacher. He saw auras of light around particular statues, the rays of the sun had a different coloring to him, and lights would even turn on by themselves. In his excitement and amazement, he wondered why events contrary to the laws of physics were happening. Did they betoken even more spectacular things to come?

In three months of waiting, not a single miracle happened. Worse than that, he encountered numerous problems both professionally and personally. He thus concluded that the "inexplicable phenomena" he had seen earlier were some freak of nature. Additionally, he began to feel there was little point in spiritual cultivation, as it neither helps you pay your bills, nor does it grant you any tangible benefit—it only accentuates your confusion and disappointment with life.

I have experienced similar experiences. Some people claim to have smelled a strong scent of sandalwood in my presence; others dreamed of me appearing as a Buddha. Some have sweated profusely and have been cured of certain ailments in my presence. There are those with "opened" third eyes who say I radiate a rainbow aura, especially while I bring forth my mantric vibrations. Such phenomena have caused certain people to get ideas about possible advantages to be gained. In a materialistic society like America, it seems that many naturally associate material benefit with spirituality.

In addressing this particular topic, I would first like to salute those who have had such remarkable experiences. Why? Because they sprout from one's divine nature. One's divine nature is like a seed buried deeply in one's heart. Once it is moistened by timely rain, it can begin to sprout. But in comparison with water, of course the seed takes precedence. It lies within one's inner nature, and needs proper nurturing to grow healthily. Thus the Buddhist tradition encourages us to turn our mindfulness inward. The word for Buddhism in Tibetan actually means "internal vision." When seeking to be awakened, if we only direct our attention outward, we will often be caught in knots of pain and confusion.

That being so, we should use wondrous events as rain to nurture our spiritual nature toward enlightenment. In this lies the ultimate purpose of such paranormal occurrences.

Once phenomenal things are emptied out, we are left with Truth. And what is Truth? I believe it has to do with using our finite earthly life to tap into the infinite, to use illusory form to approach the formless. The spheres of matter and spirit will be shown to be interchangeable and synergistic. Through this process, our spiritual nature will be elevated, and great wisdom will emerge. What pain or affliction could tie us in knots then?.

Over ten years ago, a heavenly master of mine employed paranormal powers as a special lesson for me. He had communicated to me about the unity of spirit and matter, and how they interconvert and function synergistically. Several days later, while riding my bicycle on a quiet Beijing street, I saw a woman riding six yards ahead of me, with her ten-year-old daughter sitting at the rear. Just then I felt a sensation of being touched on the crown of my head—a sign that something was about to happen. Then I witnessed the two of them, along with the bicycle, rise from the road surface and fly into sky. They made at least two loops in mid air before smoothly landing back on the road. I was astonished at such a sight, and was later told by my master that this was an example of "spirit operating on matter," which had been manifested by the master's thought waves.

On another occasion as I was walking in front of Beijing Stadium, I again felt a sensation at the crown of my head. A tall old woman appeared before me, even taller than myself. She was raggedly dressed, weather beaten, but smiling profusely. With hands crossed she walked toward me with a ludicrous rolling gait. Before I could get out of her way, she slammed into me. When I turned to look for her, she had disappeared. The master later told me that this was an "interconversion of spirit and matter," which she had manifested for my benefit. This heavenly master, with a self proclaimed age of 60,000 years, and whose name I don't know to this day, let me witness the miraculous powers of Truth.

In speaking about such wondrous events, I realize that many people will find them mysterious and hard to believe. For me, however, they were real and concrete encounters by which lessons were imparted to me. They have solidified my devotion to truth- seeking, and my faith that that absolute reality will not toy with us. Regardless of whether you believe in them or not, they do happen. The attitude of some humanist scholars of religion who wish to exclude all talk of supernatural phenomena is one-sided in my opinion. We should accept the true, compassionate intentions of bodhisattvas and enlightened beings, and not deny out of hand the things we have not experienced.

Actually, even if we pay just a little bit of attention, we will discover how unknowing and juvenile we are in the face of the natural order. We can pick out a random tree and find that it is already hundreds of years old. A simple rock holds within it messages dating back hundreds of thousands of years.

All people are equal before Creation, so there should be no distinction of superior and inferior, yet humans vary in their faculty of knowing the universe. I have chosen to share my personal story to let it be known that, in this world of great multiplicity, among people of every stripe and color, there are people who have had profound and sometimes involuntary encounters. Such paranormal occurrences have changed their perspective on life. We could say that the "skylight" has opened on our understanding of the universe. We choose to tell our stories, in hope that others will share what they see when their skylights open.

Some people have asked me what have been the tangible benefits of my awakening. My response is that the benefits are too many to list, and all are contained in the *prajna* of emptiness. The *prajna* manifested through one's empty nature is the supreme wisdom, also called root wisdom, and it goes far beyond any worldly empirical knowledge.

That one reaps what one sows is a simple idea. I have found that whenever we sow a measure of compassion, peace of mind is reaped in like measure. When we express wisdom, the return is tranquility. In tranquility and peace of mind, I have reaped a greater harvest—fearlessness and higher freedom. For someone who has experienced major sacrifices, the greatest "gift" is the wisdom of empty-naturedness. There are no gains in fame or fortune that can measure up to this great gain. For those who have passed through tempering, this gift is devoid of side effects such as pride, self- abasement and worry. The resulting spontaneity and ease of mind are benefits that cannot be measured by money.

With the guidance of friends, I visited the home of the Self Realization Fellowship in Pacific Palisades founded by Yogananda. This was my first exposure to Indic yogic practices. While we were there, we entered a classroom where several pictures were hanging. After a brief meditation, I gazed at a figure radiating concentric ripples of light. I asked my friends: "Who is the shining one?" I was quickly told that this shining deity was Krishna—called by some the foremost god of Hinduism, and identified with the supreme yogic path.

I soon found a copy of the *Bhagavad-Gita,* and it glowed with truth. It helped me understand the energetic origins of Yoga of Joy, and validated my transmission of truth. In the *Bhagavad-Gita*, the essential nature of the universe is synonymous with Krishna. Krishna also means the highest joy, in the belief that ultimate truth is also the wellspring and reservoir of all joy. The *Gita* gives a penetrating explanation of the effects of yogic practice, believing that the ultimate goal is to work with the spirit so as to set it free from material restraints. A freed spirit possesses wisdom to reach the apex of existence and be together with the Supreme Being.

The *Gita* also hints that when a certain time comes, half-divine beings will be incarnated on earth, where they will work to deliver people into the eternal realm. This reminds me of the enlightenment song Grandma left behind before entering nirvana.

One of the stanzas goes something like this:

> *All the gods, join together,*
> *to bridge humankind with Heaven.*
>
> *All the paths, awaken us,*
> *create new conditions of Buddhahood.*

On the Wings of Phoenix Rising

Real and false, false and real—
let our eyes be bright and heart aglow.

Don't be proud and spoiled,

Don't be hasty and restless,

Ride the currents of karmic cause.

— 20 —

Universal Masters

The Buddhist tradition often speaks about the realms of form and formlessness—in layman's language, the material world and the world beyond. As living beings in the realm of desire, humans focus primarily on tangible things we can use to satisfy our material needs. This world dazzles us with no end of objects to pursue. So powerful is the attraction of the earth's surface that we find it difficult to lift our heads and explore the world beyond our five physical senses. To ants that scurry about their daily labors, even a grain of rice appears amazing. Given the narrow horizons of their lives, it is difficult to envision what lies beyond.

Yet we know that all material things must go through stages of "growth, abiding, decline and dissolution." The fleshly body, with all it bonds to and relies on, is transitory and fated to disappear. Our spiritual nature, being eternal, does not experience a similar fate. Subtle entities of spirit cannot be destroyed by earthly water or fire; they do not dry up and cannot be dismembered. They can travel in and out of the material realm unhindered.

The Buddhas and bodhisattvas are elevated spiritual beings of the universe; they are the heavenly masters of humankind. They exist as high energy sources in various space-time realms, possessing the unborn and undying dharma-nature. To serve their purpose of transforming sentient beings in various spatial environments, they manifest themselves in various expedient forms, whether physical or non-physical.

Many of these high masters come from extra-dimensional planes of existence, but sometimes they enter the four-dimensional realm with which we are familiar. They come in many different ways, sometimes as light or sound, and sometimes in human form. One way or another, they manifest in forms friendly to our senses, in a manner that is convenient for us. An analogy can be drawn in our current video standards. China uses the PAL format, and in order to watch a PAL program in America, it must first be adapted to the NTSC format.

Sometimes even the minor actions of high masters will be construed as amazing events by human beings, who call such phenomena supernatural. As for people who let book knowledge define the truth for them, they may dismiss such instances as superstition.

In reality, there are mystical aspects to every religion. For instance, the Christian *Bible* is filled with miraculous occurrences. It is the same in many Buddhist sutras, where great teachers are described as radiating a magnificent light that brightens entire world systems. To "radiate" simply means that buddhas are possessed of great magnetic and compassionate energy, and with great power of understanding they can uplift sentient beings. None of this can be encompassed by mere emphasis on self-cultivation; in truth, only highly blessed and favored persons can deeply embrace this reality. It is truly fortunate to have the chance to be taught and guided by those special beings.

There have been many fortunate ones throughout history, and I count myself as one of them.

There was a time during my suicide attempts when I regarded such experiences as illusions stemming from my fascination with the supernatural. That was one of the reasons why I felt such inner torment. Now, as I look back on each wonder I have witnessed, I see that each was intended to have a cleansing and elevating effect on my life. The point was to awaken me to the phantasmal nature of ordinary reality.

Grandma's Heavenly Writing

From a very young age, I witnessed the remarkable sight of Grandma doing heavenly writing. She would first turn off the lights, saying that lamplight would blind her to her own writing. As a result, most of her heavenly writing was performed in the dark. Amazingly, her multiform inscriptions and geometrical mandalas never appeared messy or ran off the page.

She was not particular about writing materials. She would use whatever paper was available, but she would not use ballpoint pens. Her writing was usually done under one of two circumstances. The first was on my birthdays, when she would burn the inscribed slips of paper, mix the ash with water, and ask me to drink it. The second was in response to certain karmic conditions. Before the major earthquake at Tangshan,[26] I remember that she wrote several times, uttering to herself: "Write to Buddha; we need transformation and

---

26 Tangshan, a city in Shandong, is not far from Beijing. In 1976 it was at the epicenter of a 7.4 earthquake that resulted in 200,000 deaths.

guidance." Writing or drawing these heavenly communiques was completely intuitive for her, taking less than twenty seconds to finish each image or character. She never allowed us to keep these documents, except for the two that I have reproduced in this book. These were drawn prior to her departure, when she called for pen and paper to "leave a memento."

I have observed Grandma enter two different states while doing heavenly writing. The first state appeared to be a manifestation of her *alaya* consciousness,[27] which is her pure, luminous self-nature. I have heard her recall happenings from previous lifetimes upon entering this state. During one such lifetime, she gave her mother a fright by uttering "Mama" at the moment of birth. She also said that all the people in the "previous world" used the same written language, and she wrote a few examples for me to see. She also said that she had also eaten certain favorite foods in the previous world. I asked her how long ago the previous world was, and her answer surprised me. After reckoning to herself, she answered, "Thirty or forty thousand years ago at least."

Another state she wrote in was when her body, mind and speech would resonate with the empty nature of another high master. Such a master would impart non-physical energy to her mystical talismans, in order to guide and awaken a deluded mortal like myself. I mentioned earlier what happened when I complained about drinking one of her "birthday potions." As I questioned the purpose of drinking potions in an era when science had already superseded folk beliefs, my eye grew swollen and I fell mute. In the end I had to drink one

---

27 Alaya consciousness is the ground of awareness. It is sometimes called the eighth consciousness, because it underlies the five kinds of sensory consciousness, the mental consciousness, and discriminating ego consciousness. It is sometimes described as a storehouse of karmic seeds.

of Grandma's concoctions before my eye would return to normal. I am sure that anyone who has been through such an experience will not lightly trivialize such marvelous powers. Grandma herself never made much of her own writings, however. She often joked that they were not of much use. "I just like to play with them to let you know your grandmother has some culture in her yet."

What have these heavenly inscriptions done for me? Minimally, Grandma and her talismanic writings awakened my interest in prehistoric culture, opening me to the possibility of a "previous world." You can say that my mental horizons were expanded as a result. More importantly, I glimpsed how buddhas in empty space worked with non-physical energy to produce earthly effects.

Grandma was a bridge between me and all the buddhas and bodhisattvas. She was a qualified master—in fact, she smiles upon me even now from the pure land of Guanyin as I write. My grandmother, who was once restricted to a phenomenal form, has become part of the light, existing with heaven and earth, shining with the sun and the moon!

Grandma's Last Revelation to Me

It happened in October of 1989, while I was shooting a documentary in Hebei Province titled "Lost Arts of Hengshui." My mobile phone rang while I was filming Wang Xisan, an artist who paints on the inside of snuff bottles. My mother was calling to tell me that Grandma had been ill with a cold, and was refusing medical attention. She was ninety-nine years old at the time. I immediately departed from my shooting location and headed for the countryside where she had been living—Grandma did not enjoy city life, and was spending her advanced years in the countryside. When I saw her, she appeared weak and her throat seemed congested. She coughed and gently said to me: "Your aunt made some very salty dumplings for me. Even my organs feel salty right now." As I began to cry, she put a finger on my tears and tasted it, saying: "All the salt I have eaten is now pouring out of you...I will be fine with a little more sleep."

She spent some time composing herself before asking me: "Where is the 'black hair' that you gave me?" (I had given her a black velvet hat, which she called her 'black hair.') "Please bring it to me; I want to take a picture." Saying this, she shakily stood up, and with my assistance went out to the backyard and stood for her final photograph. After I took the picture, she returned back to her room and asked everyone to be quiet. We heard some minor coughing through her door, and then her breathing grew even. Two hours later, she began to breathe heavily. The doctor we called wanted to give her an injection, but although he bent a needle trying, he could not penetrate her blood vessels. Then her breathing grew very faint. Mother and the other family members began to pray in the other room.

Someone suggested that we should ask at the altar if it would be possible to keep Grandma longer. Mother made a bundle of incense sticks, lit them, and prayed: "Must my mother leave us? I am willing to give years from my lifespan to keep her longer." Before she even finished with this prayer, the bundle of brightly burning incense went out with a whoosh, as if an invisible knife had cut through it. Mother did not give up, and continued to plead three more times, each time with the same result. Only then did it sink in that Grandma was leaving us, and we began to consider her funeral arrangements.

As Grandma lay on the bed with a faint smile on her face, I held a stick of incense near her nostrils and detected that she was still breathing. Suddenly, I saw that she had floated up in mid air and was waving at me. I looked on the bed for her, and saw that now there were two of her. Both had the same physical characteristics, down to the clothes. The difference was that the Grandma in midair had an animated expression, with an aura around her body. Meanwhile the column of incense smoke was blown aside at intervals, which showed that the Grandma in bed was breathing. Then Grandma in midair began to speak to me. She did not actually speak; rather, her words were spoken through my mouth: "It is now time. I must return. You shall not cry, or burn paper money, or bow to every visitor. Don't make a big ceremony, I like quiet." Finishing her final instructions, she disappeared from midair.

Meanwhile the Grandma on the bed was still breathing. Once again I trained my gaze into mid air to look for her. I saw a new image of her, now dressed in a shimmering golden gown. Her hair was glossy black, and her features were those of a young woman. She was being led into a huge palace in which colorful clouds were visible. She appeared curious as she delightedly surveyed her new abode. Her face even showed a shy expression as her fingers played over her new clothes. Suddenly, the image changed: she was now sitting opposite Guanyin, listening intently...

I then heard Mother's voice off in the distance: "Mother is gone!" I pulled myself back from the visions and saw that the incense smoke near Grandmother's nostrils was ascending straight up—she had stopped breathing.

This was such a beautiful scene! In most external ways, Grandmother had been quite ordinary—she had neither fame, fortune, nor materialistic enjoyments. You will not find her name in newspapers or important texts. However, her right views, right beliefs, and right conduct afforded her an extraordinarily graceful and composed exit from this world. By witnessing her final moments, I was able to verify for myself the Buddha-realms described in sacred texts.

Guanyin Bodhisattva

In my spiritual journey, it has been revealed to me that Guanyin Bodhisattva is a very great master among the high masters of the universe. Beginning when I was three years old, she has appeared in various forms before me: a kindly lady dressed in ancient garb, a Buddha-mother surrounded by rings of light, a white-clad adept, an ornately dressed queen, a humble holy mother, a voice within an aura surrounding a silver dragon, the goddess of Mt. Tai, an elderly boatman, Green Tara, or perhaps a farm lady. Of the many forms she has appeared in, she has manifested most frequently as light. I believe that light is the real form of Guanyin, for her nature is emptiness, and as such partakes of infinite energy stored in the highest level of the cosmos, which is free to manifest itself in particular realms and states. These manifestations transform time and space, exceeding the speed of light by virtue of the Buddha's power.

Guanyin is the primordial Buddha. She is transcendent super energy abiding as long as the universe abides. Her heavenly dwelling is among the highest heavenly bodies, and many people on earth today actually come from her realm. As it is written in one sutra, "After the initial completion of the world, heavenly beings of light and vibration shall descend, each of them surrounded by light..." Because of our unique karmic association with Guanyin, she calls and reaches out to us like a mother to her children, using numerous paths of convenience to transform all sentient beings.

In Tibetan Buddhism, Guanyin has many emanations. One of them is the Zhun-ti Buddha-Mother. Zhun-ti means "linked by silken ropes;" another translation is "clear" or "numinous," a meaning that embraces countless buddha-mothers as well as the buddhas of past, present and future. "Linked by silken ropes" implies that the Buddha-Mother saves sentient beings with ropes of compassion, connecting with them by the strength of her vows. The word *prajna* means supreme wisdom. In the *Heart Sutra* we find this line: "Buddhas of the past, present and future, by means of *prajnaparamita*, obtain supreme enlightenment." Both the Zhun-ti Buddha-Mother and the Prajna Buddha-Mother express supreme Dharma-nature. Other emanations that come to mind are female bodhisattvas such as Four-Armed Guanyin, Six-Armed Guanyin, Ten-Faced Guanyin, the Auspicious Heavenly Mother, the Twenty-one Taras, the Red Bodhisattva of Oceanic Compassion, the Mother of the Compassionate Canopy, the Buddha-Mother Dingji-Zunsheng, the Lion-Faced Sunyata Mother, and the Jixiang Tianshou Regal Mother. I think that no matter how many mandalic images or names are attributed to the Guanyin who is coextensive with all space, these are just another arm or eye among her thousands of arms and eyes. They are representations exhibited for the benefit of all sentient beings.

Thus I strongly believe this line from the *Diamond Sutra:* "Do not try to seek me through form, for all forms are in vain." I construe this to mean that the Buddha is an extremely elevated form of "knowing" and "energy" who pervades all of empty space and the dharma-realm, without form or physical substance, without traces or shadows. I also enjoy the *Heart Sutra* very much. In this concise sutra, you cannot find a particular reference to compassion, but you can feel the immense compassionate intention behind the words. It is pared down to the essence, and therein lies abundance. From nothing comes something, and that something is a reminder, an instruction, a persuasion, and a calling. *"Tadjatha, Om, Gate gate, paragate, parasamgate, bodhi-svaha."*[28]

I am reminded of an experience of mine that will further illustrate, in a more accessible manner, the infinite compassion of Guanyin. This event happened sometime around 1988, when I befriended an American couple. The husband's name was David, and the wife was Julie. Both of them came from Ohio, but at the time they were teaching English at a Chinese university. Julie had not been feeling well, and decided to return to America early. She informed me of her decision, and I wanted to give her a uniquely Chinese gift for her departure.

I went to shop for Julie at an arts and crafts store, and saw a cloisonne Guanyin holding a water vessel, that I thought would make a meaningful gift. But then I thought that since Julie was not familiar with bodhisattvas, she probably would not like such a present. I then picked out a pair of bracelets that were also quite suitable. As I walked out of the store with the bracelets, an immaterial hand seemed to press strongly on my head, so much so that it spun my body around. Involuntarily, I walked back to the counter and stared directly at the Guanyin statue. Needless to say, I purchased the Guanyin and gave it to Julie as a parting gift.

After several days had passed, David called through a translator,

---

[28] This mantra, which concludes the Heart Sutra, was rendered by D. Suzuki as: "Gone, gone, gone to the other shore, landed at the other shore, Ah bliss of awakening!" This Sutra, numbering less than 300 words, is a distillation of teachings about prajna.

saying that he had an important question to ask me. After they arrived, David informed me that Julie's flight had encountered serious turbulence, to the point that all passengers were instructed to wear life vests, and be prepared for a possible crash landing. Amidst the general panic, Julie remembered the water-sprinkling Guanyin in her carrying case, so she took it out and prayed to it. After her prayer, she saw a white-clad Guanyin appear outside the plane, directing it toward safety. Quickly thereafter the turbulence stopped, and everyone calmed down.

Immediately after getting off the flight, Julie called David to tell him about this very unique experience. She also asked two questions: First, the Guanyin that I gave her wore blue, yet the Guanyin she saw wore white. Why was that? And second, Guanyin is a goddess of the Chinese people; why did she protect an American who knew nothing about her?

Who Is Jesus?

Julie's experience strengthened my faith and devotion to Guanyin, but also raised some questions. I wanted to know, for instance, what Christianity is? Why is it that so many Christians seem to dislike Buddhists? Who is Jesus? Is he God? These were big questions, and whatever information I found in books could not answer them completely.

I also went to Fujian Province that year and stayed at Xiamen University, not far from the famed Southern Putuo Temple. My local host was a devout Christian, and was not aware of my spiritual beliefs or experiences. During that particular period, Putuo Temple was enjoying a period of robust attendance and worship. Many devoted believers arrived each morning at the temple doors, bearing all types of gifts. Not being familiar with such practices, I closely examined the writing on the offerings out of curiosity. Many prayer wishes, such as "fast pregnancy with son," "smooth road to wealth," or "luck against all odds" were written on the various gifts presented to the temple.

My friend said derisively: "This is Buddhism! Many of these people have committed evil acts, and do not want to suffer the legal consequences, so they come here pleading for Buddha's mercy! Others have come from Taiwan, and are on their second or third concubine, and they are hoping to father a son. They too wish to be blessed. This level of faith is too lowly for me!" At that time I also felt rather disquieted by my observations. These believers were projecting their desirous "faith" onto desireless buddhas. They believed that they could use money and gifts to curry favor with the Buddha. These superstitious practices really belong to the category of folk customs and not to a spiritual path. I told my friend that I understood her point of view, and expressed my distaste as well. She was pleased that I agreed with her, and used that opportunity to invite me to attend a special Christian service with her.

The night before the service, I spoke to Guanyin Bodhisattva in my heart: "I shall go listen to a Christian minister preach tomorrow. Please tell me who Jesus is? Why is it that he has many believers, and has such a long tradition?" At dawn the next day, I saw a special scene. Against the constellations of stars, a very large, bright and colorful star stood out plainly. I heard a female voice in the air: "A great, great Bodhisattva." An indescribable feeling of bliss overtook me.

Being the first person to arrive at Church, I sat in the first row, quite close to the female pastor. A gentle light surrounded her body, so I knew she had been enveloped by the "holy spirit." She spoke of Jesus being born in a manger, to express that the Lord was not proud or ego-centered. He was born with equal love for all... I enjoyed hearing this message full of sincerity and love. I took the message to heart, combining it with many personal encounters, and a clear signal emerged: Within the range of spatial dimensions in the universe, there exist many heavenly realms. These are sometimes called heavenly kingdoms or spheres. Within every one of these realms and spheres are heavenly bodies bearing life forms with varying levels of wisdom and power. These various higher life forms live in higher dimensions of the non-physical universe.

Such higher life forms are not only non-physical, they can even be considered "anti-matter." Their luminous bodies exist in the void, free to gather and disperse, without borders or boundaries. Their lives may span tens of thousands of years or countless eons. Some of them, by our modern interpretation, are what people call extraterrestrials. Many of them grow by absorbing consciousness, so they have wisdom; they are embodied in light, so they can come and go freely. They are a special type of radiant energy—a highly refined and ethereal type of energy. To them, the human race is one big family whose fates are inextricably intertwined, unseparated by rank. Not only that, human lives are also deeply connected with all the heavenly life forms. Accordingly, the precious buddhas have taught us the underlying unity and equality of sentient beings. Christian doctrine also teaches the similar idea of universal love. Such ideals come to us by illumination from beings that we choose to call buddhas or bodhisattvas, or God. Such illumination is the essential nature and the overarching order of the universe.

Proof of the multiplicity of the universe is being put forth, in preliminary form, by scientists working within their own fields of inquiry. Some of these scientists are Christians, others Buddhists; some are without a spiritual tradition altogether. Many have been led to remarkable conclusions based on their own experiential findings. These experiences transcend many religious doctrines; they transcend the narrow, long-held tenets of *anthropic cosmology*.[29] In the 21st Century, there will be more people who transcend the confines of religion to experience and realize Truth directly. The understanding that results from this will have a deep impact on world peace.

There are many different heavenly realms in the universe. It has been said in Buddhist texts that "all worlds follow karmic dispositions as they come to be" and "these are inhabited by the sentient beings of countless buddha-fields." People have created names for the beings in these various realms: gods, buddhas, immortals, angels, arhats, heavenly beings, etc. Different realms in space are interconnecting and interdependent. According to their degree of ethereality, they occupy varying levels of existence. As such, there are distinctions in their ways of life.

Some deities live by absorbing whatever it is that makes up space. Some heavenly beings that have a close association with earthlings may use incense fumes as nourishment. The guardian deities of Buddhism, for instance, are such beings, and I have personally experienced their presence. In Beijing, it is customary to burn a certain type of mosquito-repellant incense. One time, without thinking, I

---

[29] This cosmological argument suggests that the physical conditions of the Earth, such as its oxygen content and distance from the Sun, are not inadvertently beneficial to intelligent life, but might actually be specially fine-tuned for life. This has been slow to gain acceptance among scientists because anthropic logic seems disregard the fact that the universe was here long before man evolved.

burned a coil of such incense close to the family altar. That particular evening, a guardian deity that was passing through said aloud: "What is that terrible smell?"

This particular incident gave me insight into the incense- and fire-related ceremonies in Tibetan Buddhism. In fact, such practices can be found in many world religions. Many guardian deities rely on incense to identify the objects of their solicitude. The lighting of incense, coupled with the motivation and intention of the believer, constitute a special message that can be directed toward a particular deity or guardian. In the same way, negative motivations and intentions will attract beings of lesser purity, resulting in an outcome that may not be very positive. This is another reason why all religions value inner states of wisdom and compassion.

The Buddhist path emphasizes the cultivation of one's heart. The higher and purer one's heart becomes, the easier it is to connect with higher levels of energy, resulting in better guidance and direction from above. With this understanding, one naturally realizes that with upright thoughts and motivations, one will not be unduly harmed or disturbed by negative spiritual forces. In other words, beliefs held in the heart come naturally equipped with strong protective force. Coarser and lower energy sources, in the presence of someone pure in heart, will actually be purified or lessened. This is another reason why beings of pure light, such as buddhas, have the capacity to save or elevate sentient beings. If one accepts these actualities, there is no need to act like Ye Gong the *dragon fancier*,[30] letting ourselves be startled by "supernatural phenomena" beyond the five senses. The buddhas will bless those who face these occurrences calmly, who

---

[30] Legend has it that Ye Gong was so interested in dragons that he surrounded himself with images of them, but when he finally saw a dragon for himself, he was frightened half to death.

handle them with wisdom and sublimate them to a higher level.

In the tantric tradition we speak of Vairocana Buddha, also called Tathagata of the Great Sun, whose realization placed him in an extremely high realm. This Buddha's principal path is to empower people's hearts with his magical abilities. Thus the full tide of the *Great Sun Sutra* is the *Sutra of Vairocana's Magical Empowerments*. Bookish people only give credence to the cultivation techniques and philosophical message of Buddhism, while true believers become overzealous about the possibility of certain miraculous powers. In truth both groups have a skewed perspective. To the higher life forms of the universe, notions of a "supernatural" realm simply do not exist, for everything is natural. What we describe as supernatural today is merely the sky as described by a frog at the bottom of a well.

The masters of the universe are "super" life-forms that exist within emptiness, yet possess infinite energy. They represent ultimate realization and an absolute order. We cultivate ourselves and follow the path of spirit, so we can get closer to their realm of Truth. In doing so, we meld with the universal order.

These are 'heavenly writings' left by my Grandma. "When the time comes, you will understand them."

Several people have shown an interest in probing the meaning of Grandma's 'heavenly writings.' Some shapes remind them of yoga positions, geometric figures, and constellations.

21

How to Receive Guidance from Heavenly Masters

The doorway to Truth is inherently formless, but forms and regimens have accumulated over thousands of years of human endeavor. How can we transcend form, and raise our sights from self-made barriers so our life can encompass a greater vision? This leads into the next topic of discussion, which is how one can experience true reality more directly, and how one can align more closely with heavenly masters so as to benefit from their guidance.

This is a process of adjusting your life's frequency and bandwidth. If you feel attracted to this possibility, please consider the following lessons as grist for your mill, and put them in practice.

Real Adepts Converse about Daily Matters

Truth is not a luxury adornment for one's facade—it is not something to spice up your humdrum days, nor is it a miracle cure for life's inevitable reversals. Truth will not put on a show to satisfy seekers of adventure or excitement. The unadorned Truth seems to be without particular color or flavor, but when you enter it, you find deep within an abundance of wonderful scenery. To fully appreciate its wondrous beauty, you must begin with simplicity. As such, one need not direct attention and energy toward an exquisite altar, nicely bound books, an ornate lecture room, or the number of times you have visited holy sites in India or Tibet. The highest realm in which to seek the Way is simplicity.

With simplicity as the foundation for one's practice, it is natural to distance oneself from the illusory world of high-flown talks and debates, to be detached from the shallowness of deluded achievement. The meaning of "real adepts converse about daily matters" is that genuine seekers convey an air of humility, as if they can only speak of everyday matters. Simplicity of heart and the strength to bear loneliness complement each other, giving rise to inner composure and "thunderous silence."

"Thunderous silence" means quieting the body, abiding in a clear, relaxed state; it means quieting speech that is empty, false and idle, so as not to scatter one's transformative focus; it means quieting inner confusion, to let consciousness abide in an illumined, transcendent state; it means to quiet one's senses, to keep from overindulging in material wants; it means quieting one's behavior, so it is natural and without contrived drama. Only in this way can one build up *sunyata* mastery. *Sunyata* mastery is transcendent power exercised in empty-naturedness by heavenly masters.

From Non-Grasping Comes Spiritual Resonance

First, simply let yourself live, without unnecessary complications.

Many people become attached to accumulation of wealth, only to dull their awareness of impermanence. Many self-proclaimed financial or management experts, as seen from the perspective of eternity, are not keeping their ledgers clearly. Depositing all one's hopes and aspirations into a bank that will ultimately go bankrupt, namely that of impermanence, will surely earn "dividends" in the form of ignorance and attachment. The more of these dividends one builds up, the more obstacles are created. After one exhales his last breath, such a life must come to a helter-skelter conclusion.

Of course, each person faces different circumstances, and each stands to fail or succeed in his own way. One "accomplishment" that we are all heading toward, however, is our inevitable death. In the face of this, all other accomplishments appear inconsequential. Are we not foolish to smash the fragile egg of illusory greed and attachment against the solid rock of death's reality?

Grasping comes first in the list of five evils in the Buddhist tradition. From the soil of grasping sprouts the poisonous weeds of hatred, delusion, pride and suspicion. Grasping ones calculate everything they do from a perspective of personal gain and loss. There is a Tibetan saying: "In the eyes of a cow, even the most beautiful flower is nothing but a tuft of grass." Sometimes, grasping even emerges because of empowerment by heavenly masters. One may calculate the monetary worth of this flower called empowerment, tallying up dividends against investment. By attaching to the minor self, grasping narrows one's mental horizons, leading one to doubt and even deride the underlying reality of life.

Grasping for wealth, sex or fame is born from illusions created by our sensory and mental faculties. Since coming to America, I have noticed what I call the "passive absorption syndrome" due to information overload. There is an abundance of information on Eastern mysticism, because it is one of the streams that feeds into the New Age movement. Because of their personal predicaments, seekers are looking for something, and they can easily be infected with this condition. Chances to gratify curiosity are hard to resist, so they read and accumulate massive amounts of knowledge, which only make them feel increasingly weak and hollow inside. The end result is an overactive mouth that espouses plausible doctrine, yet takes no action.

There are indeed very valuable teachings to be found in ancient Chinese culture that address this predicament. For instance, it is said at the outset in the *Dao De Jing,* "The Tao that can be told is not the eternal Tao; the name that can be named is not the eternal Name." Sages and wise men of antiquity coined expressions such as "The Tao begins where language ends." This saying basically means that the highest forms of wisdom and Truth need not have expression in language.

Now I see many people engulfed in whirlpools of information who cannot find their way to the vast ocean of truth. Those afflicted by this "passive absorption syndrome" are bound to develop indigestion, resulting in loss of appetite for spiritual food. This is because they have encountered grasping teachers or friends; at the same time, they expose themselves to copious information without knowing how to simplify them.

The antidote to greed is letting go. Letting go of grasping is letting go of attachment. Without attachment, a natural fearlessness develops. From this fearlessness emerges a natural state of calm and relaxation. To be truly calm and relaxed is to rest in a soft and pliable state without forced action or thought of gain. This is because one has departed from the "rat race" of status, and withdrawn from judgmental conflicts. Naturally this does not mean giving up normal work or arrangements for daily life. The Eightfold Noble Path taught by the Buddha Sakyamuni includes the item "right livelihood." Right livelihood, which is also called "right exertion," is not used for power plays or self-glorification. Rather, it should be in service of genuine living. Right exertion, therefore, is also the appropriate exertion. The right exertion is like the calm ocean surface that is open to the passage of large and small vessels alike. All worldly things should be as such.

When grasping is gone, the power of other poisons—hatred, delusion, pride and suspicion—is also lessened. With the mind's capacity enlarged, we become more like the sky, like the ocean, with space to nurture sincerity and abundance. At that time, we will receive a true dividend—joy and, emerging from it, the various transformational games between matter and spirit. The heavenly masters can then be invited to partake in this dance. Do not worry, the masters will join, as long as they are not summoned in a grasping spirit.

Innocence Is Fertile Soil

The innocence we speak of is the result of self-cultivation. The childish naivete that some believe to be innocence comes from inexperience, but innocence that arises from maturity is the expression of wisdom. Innocence is clarity that comes from penetrating into reality, an expression of the true self. The innocent will not give undue emphasis to orthodoxy or external knowledge, for when external logic and knowledge become lodged internally, the result will be obstacles and partial truths. As such, the innocent rely on direct awareness to gain a full understanding of causal processes. With no need for detours through conventionality or power relations, they arrive straight at the underlying Truth. Thus innocence is energy; it is evolutionary; it is unassuming wisdom.

Innocence of character does not trade love as a commodity. It does not tally up advantages with finicky precision; it will not seek the Truth with one hand while holding a calculator in the other. An innocent person's unmuddied vision takes in reality as a whole; he goes out to meet the world with a trusting childlike heart.

Innocence is the blessed shore on which we land after living through trials and tribulations. Heavenly masters cherish this quality, for they too are absolutely innocent!

No-Gate Is the Dharma Gate

Do not grasp after connections or limit yourself to a particular path, for doing so may plunge you into partisanship and separation. Universal consciousness lets all things gather and disperse naturally within its implicate order. But a person's thoughts must not be allowed to disperse. A scattered mind is like a thin cloud that easily disperses in even the smallest wind.

Before one achieves indestructible *prajna*-wisdom, it is important to have something to abide in. Just as a tree abides in a forest, and even the strongest winds do not uproot an entire forest, we all need a community of spiritual refuge. Such refuge is a remedy emerging from emptiness, which integrates our scattered hearts. Thus it is important to settle upon a certain universal master, to whom we give a particular name, because many universal masters have grown accustomed to their names over time.

In the Buddhist tradition, for instance, it is said that to respect one Buddha is to respect all Buddhas. That is to say, a particular form of reverence and abidance can be, at the same time, an all-embracing faith. One can abide in Guanyin, in various deities, in Jesus and the Holy Mother. One should pray with devotion, whether in adversity or celebration, and always without doubtfulness. At the same time, keep your heart open. Do not use Guanyin to belittle this god or that deity, and do not create a competitive situation between the Buddha and Jesus. Do not use one scripture to dismiss another. In this way, you will have the wisdom to absorb essential truths of all paths and religions.

Opening yourself does not mean running after externals, going to a dharma assembly today, to India tomorrow, and to Tibet the day after. Abiding with the high masters only takes focus and deep mindfulness. It does not require a lot of money or time.

I have known people who spout many words on spiritual matters and suppose themselves to be enlightened. In truth, their enlightenment is still at an earthly level. For a thorough awakening to life beyond birth, old age, sickness and death, one must acknowledge the higher forms of life in the universe as masters. Life in higher dimensions has "broadened their horizons" and given them wisdom free from afflictions. We must in all humility seek them out as masters. Oftentimes, we talk of spirit without truly abiding in anything. This results in a blurred faith that does not show itself in our lives, is not directed or guided. It is therefore important for one to experience complete faith through abidance in specific masters.

In the Tibetan tantric tradition, this type of cultivation is sometimes called deity yoga, heavenly yoga, or guru yoga. In principle, tantra owes its unparalleled power to the way it emphasizes cultivation of guru yoga, founded on full understanding of empty-naturedness. When one contemplates by means of empty-natured *prajna* only, without guru yoga, the pace of maturation may be slower.

The only preparation needed to abide with a master is to make the mind utterly sincere. Just as rays of sunlight can be harnessed by a magnifying glass to ignite a fire, a pure sincere heart uses power from the masters to eradicate ignorance and afflictions.

It is important to make room for the masters at any time in your silent heart-space. Depending on your particular habits and likes, you can choose from a variety of ways to make this space possible. In your moment of silence, your body and mind are pliant and suffused with clarity. Your channel nodes and the entire bio-energy system (the seven chakras) are open and flexible. The finite is released to the infinite. In this state, you emit a subtler frequency that puts you immediately in touch with the universal masters.

The Great Dao Embraces the World

This point brings us back to my grandmother. During the Cultural Revolution in China, all of Grandma's relatives were persecuted to some extent because of Grandfather's execution as a reactionary Buddhist ringleader. For many of them, life was filled with hopelessness and depression. Even my uncle (married to one of Grandma's daughters), who served as a minor official in the government, was severely treated on account of his association with our family. Oftentimes, the relatives would all get together to commiserate with each other.

On one occasion, my aunt complained to Grandma: "Every day we have to chant slogans like 'Long live *so-and-so!*' But after all the wrongs they have committed, why should they rule forever?"

Grandma responded: "They are just like all sentient beings. Our family has a karmic tie with all sentient beings, not a hateful relationship. There is no reason you can't come to terms with your father's death. Even the great sage Milarepa, after reaching the peak of his cultivation, was poisoned to death. You must not evaluate things from a common worldly perspective. If your father had stayed alive, and continued to be a "great master" receiving offerings from thousands of followers, all of you children would have become prideful and conceited. It is fitting the way things worked out. You have to bow your head down so you can learn to be humble and place others before yourselves. This is a great lesson! As for the People's Liberation Army, it is made up of nothing but a bunch of children. They don't even understand the essence of Buddhism. Who knows, perhaps many of them will be awakened one day. The Buddha that resides within the heart cannot be destroyed by vandals. This is also a test for the Tibetans, to prove the purity of their faith."

I have heard many such discourses from Grandma. Many people have an equally difficult time understanding why it is that Guanyin, in her infinite wisdom, could not prevent the Dalai Lama from going into exile. Grandma's perspective was that the snowy highlands of Tibet had been specially chosen by Guanyin, which is why people there can chant *"Om Mane Padme Hum"*[31] practically the moment they are born. There are many adepts and realized ones in Tibet, and their karma has destined them for different outcomes. Some remain in Tibet to continue their teachings, some travel to the interior of China, while others, including the Dalai Lama and his students, have

---

[31] Om-mane-padme-hum is Guanyin Bodhisattva's great mantra of illumination. All Tibetan people know this mantra.

been directed toward the West. This way of being "directed" can be likened to a dramatic play, with the Dalai Lama "making an escape" from China, and then going from India onto the world stage. The Dalai Lama gained the concern and sympathy of Western countries, and in the process proclaimed the Buddha teachings. It is easy to see that without this set of circumstances, few people would have had the chance to come in contact with the wonderful spiritual traditions of Tibet—a land long closed to the outside world. The role played by the Dalai Lama in this incarnation is one of an exile sounding a hopeful message of global peace.

Grandma spoke of things that I could not immediately grasp. Now, I understand them all. From a multitude of external forms she brought to life a larger purpose: to open and deepen the scope of compassion, and extend the reach of love higher and wider. Her personal evolution had reached a point of not judging, dividing, and labeling phenomena. She had gotten past conceptual morality to arrive at wisdom. During difficult times when most religious believers, to ease their suffering and reinforce their sense of justice, would have prayed for God to punish the evildoers, Grandma quietly stood her ground. She was devoid of anger, hatred and combativeness. She remained calm in the face of disaster, and manifested the quality of emerging from mud without stain.

I recall my uncle's perplexed face. He would exclaim: "You sure can handle hardship." Her response was: "If one is to save others from hardship, it is important to be able to endure hardship oneself. Only then will a heart of true compassion emerge..."

I received a revelation from her: Life throws rough circumstances toward us, and only wisdom can resolve their meaning. When we are tested by Heaven, there is a reason. Whether we can view each obstacle as a blessing, whether every "bad" person we encounter is a messenger, depends on whether our hearts are with the Dao, and whether our love truly reaches high and deep. We can retrieve something worthwhile out of karma, but only if we make offerings in spirit even to forces we perceive as negative. We should give thanks for the wonderful opportunity to be tested, which enables us to develop patience and compassion.

The Dao that embraces the world is not displayed in external qualities. It is to be graceful but not proud, passionate but not compulsive, calm but not cold, sincere but not attached. There is a poem that I enjoy very much: "Heaven does not speak of its height; Earth does not boast of its depth. The fuller the grain on the stalk, the lower it bows." Big love is like the full grain on the stalk, humbly bowing its head. Big love is wisdom; it is a conduit through which the universal masters seek their own. Their children's inner world is always selfless and abundant.

— 22 —

A Great Prophecy

A special message was inserted in the flyleaf of this book's first Chinese edition: "Yoga of Joy is not only a form of yoga, it will also lead to a bright calling." I invited those who are karmically associated to be involved with our planning and activities. Within a few short months, many companions have appeared just at the right time. In our discussions, we have all felt the guiding hand of a certain calling. We even joked that a plot had been woven around some of us. No one can say for sure exactly when this "plot" began. My sense of conviction dates back to 1985, around the time of the visitation by light globes. At that time, I received only a very simple message that I would go to America in the future. As to what I would do in America, the message was silent. I remember that my aunt was indignant over this disclosure; she believed that Grandma was showing favoritism and wanted me to indulge myself in America. Even back then, Grandma explained that this was a plan set forth by Guanyin.

Many events in my life since 1985 have been narrated in earlier chapters. Through over fifteen years of living and dying, coming and going, I had forgotten about coming to America. Perhaps instead of "forgetting" it would be more accurate to say that I did not care, that I had no wish to go to America. My job in CCTV's international department gave me access to foreign films and plenty of opportunities for international travel; English classes at all levels were also offered for staff members. But none of those avenues to America appealed to me, because I did not have the inclination. You could say my state of mind was one of passive resistance. In truth, my life in Beijing left me very little desire for life in a foreign land. More importantly, I did not know what I could possibly accomplish.

It wasn't until Spring Festival of 1999, when Guanyin appeared and guided me to "leave everything and go to America," followed by matching developments in the worldly sphere, that I was shocked into recognizing the "inescapable net of Dharma." This entire process was swift, clear and precise. It was a matter of "Heaven urging, Earth exhorting, and human ties pushing" that caused me to come to America. In reality the stage, or trap, had been set since my birth, or perhaps even earlier. When I was three years old, Guanyin had already appeared to foreshadow that after growing up I would go forth with an empty vase seeking to be schooled by her. I do not know whether I am completely grown up, but indeed, since that time, my understanding of the emptiness in that empty vase has grown. Now I am venturing forth as I did when I left home at age three, empty bottle in hand, step by step, being led aboard the *Dharma-ship* of the bodhisattvas.

What am I here to accomplish in America? Aside from completing my own cultivation, am I here simply to teach Yoga of Joy?

In America I can see that yoga is quite a popular occupation that is quickly gaining acceptance within the mainstream. Tantric yoga, in particular, is something many people are strongly interested in learning about. But this is not my only calling either. My calling comes from a great prophecy, and Yoga of Joy is only part of it.

On November 11, 1999, my American friends called to say they would purchase a ticket for my trip to America. The *Dharma-ship* was nearing the shore, but to me it was like "viewing flowers in the mist." For one thing, I felt unsure about certain friends connected with this project, because "desire had turned them to the path of wisdom." They were thus spurred to play the role of catalyst, but I would turn out to be someone quite different from their expectations.

That evening I did an extra-long session of yoga, to seek direct counsel from Guanyin. My high master once again confirmed her instructions: *"Leave everything behind and go to America."*

I then asked, "What shall I do in America?"

The answer: *"A Foundation."*

Question: "The name?"

Answer: *"The New Century Foundation."*

Question: "What shall this organization do?" (asked three times).

Answer: *"The apex of human civilization is created upon the merging of Eastern and Western cultures. At that time, heavenly bodies shall be aligned with the Great Pyramids and other spectacular structures."*

Another question: "What time will that be realized?"

Answer: *"In the year 2050, human beings shall arrive at an unprecedented culture."*

At this point some readers, not unlike myself, will surely be set to wondering and imagining. This is without doubt a great prophecy, and the date is not too far in the future. The younger ones among us can even personally experience that cultural apex, and view the wondrous sight of convergent energies causing heavenly bodies to align with magnificent earthly structures. As far as the rich, specific content of this coming cultural apex, everyone will have the right to explain and solve this mystery. Here, I would like to put forth my offering in that vein, to stimulate more fruitful viewpoints: the people of the new century, under guidance of the Heavenly eye, the Dharma eye, who will engage in a great transformation of consciousness. This transformation will converge out of a state of great tumult and dispersion. An overriding karmic law will resolve the disorder, and consciousness will redeem the workings of matter through immaterial power. Every sentient being will play a leading role in this transformation. Every science and every religion will advance beyond their existing confines. Within a vast, deep vision they will commune across their divisions, until intellect is liberated and they accept the pure Truth.

Under the guidance of the heavenly masters, the *New Century Foundation* has already been created. This is an international organization, currently based in California, that seeks to build bridges of greater cultural understanding between East and West. The foundation is engaged in three principal areas of work:

1. Creation of Joyful Healing Centers
2. Production of media programs aimed at exploration and exposition of Truth.
3. Utilization of Internet, audio and video programs, books, and broadcast channels to conduct East-West

cultural exchanges at a fundamental level. This includes aspects of new Western spirituality that are of proven value.

I would like to emphasize here that I have boundless concern for China. China is the home to almost 1.4 billion people, nearly a quarter of the world's population. China has 56 ethnic groups, and its cultural heritage spans over 5,000 years. It has many sacred Buddhist sites such as Tibet; it has Taoism. It is the home of sages and adepts ranging from Tsungkhapa,[32] Padmasambhava and Milarepa[33] to Laozi, the Sixth Chan Patriarch,[34] and Bodhidharma.[35] The majority of Chinese people are good-hearted and intelligent, but overpopulation and political movements have thrown this ancient nation off balance, especially in the spiritual and mental realm. According to recent statistics compiled by the Beijing Health Department, all of its mental health facilities are severely overcrowded, and inadequate care has deepened the crisis of those afflicted with mental disorders. There is a crisis of faith and healthy spirituality in China, which has resulted in many other social problems. But even such challenges cannot keep China from being fertile ground that will bear abundant fruit in the 21st Century. What is needed is for seeds to be sown, and

---

32 Tsungkhapa (1357-1419) was a great Tibetan teacher who was thought to be an incarnation of Manjusri Bodhisattva. He established a definitive curriculum for the monastic universities and founded the Great Miracle Prayer Festival in Lhasa. He wrote a master treatise on Buddhist thought entitled Great Stages on the Path.

33 Milarepa, who lived in Tibet during the eleventh and twelfth centuries, is thought of by Tibetan Buddhists as an exemplar of yogic accomplishment. His poems have been translated as the Hundred Thousand Songs of Milarepa.

34 The Sixth Patriarch Huineng (d. 713) was the most influential teacher of Chan Buddhism in China. All major Chan lineages, including the Lin-ji and Cao-dong Schools, emerged from his line of disciples.

35 Bodhidharma was a Buddhist teacher from India whose arrival in China during the Liang dynasty marked the beginning of Chan Buddhism in China.

for this sowing to be done during the season of rain. On this matter I have tremendous faith— that under nature's order and laws, China's huge population will not be left out. Here, I sincerely invite all who share this vision to involve themselves with the work and mission of the New Century Foundation—to manifest your wisdom and love.

— 23 —

Who Am I in the Infinite Game?

As my story comes to a close, a question that has hovered just out of reach remains to be answered, and that is, who am I in the endless continuum of existence? In the great game that encompasses this world and the other world, what role do I play?

In the short time that I have been in America, I have grown in experience and wisdom. Many lifelong seekers have taken an interest in me, and for all their experience, many still find it hard to place me in an understandable context, for I am unlike the familiar characters they have come across. In fact, I like the newness that this experience brings, and I join their ranks in objectively and coolly observing this Yuan Miao on her stage. What is this "performance" all about?

Who am I? That is both a simple and complex question. Perhaps I can begin by addressing who I am not.

First, I am not a strict adherent to orthodoxy or a researcher who studies various religious cultures. I am not a member of any particular sect. I believe that solid doing is born of real knowing, and that realizations are found and validated within an underlying reality. If thousands of spiritual paths exist, I believe every one of them can be doorways leading into the kingdom of Truth, so long as we listen faithfully to our intuitions and experiences.

An encompassing perfection is often spoken of in the Buddhist tradition, but actually this belief has given rise to many different sects. Although "non-discrimination" is considered an elevated state, many discriminate for or against without realizing it. Many paths are touted as the pure path, and out of that belief, many heretical paths also appear. Ultimately, a highly developed philosophical methodology is not the same as simple knowing. The complexity and competitiveness between paths have already scared many people off the path altogether. Given the collective karma and root capacities of people in the 21st Century, I believe we require a simpler, more expedient way. We also need a broader, further-reaching field of vision.

I am not a critic, and am equipped with neither the interest nor the ability to offer criticism. In my view, all spiritual paths enjoy a synergistic relationship in which one inevitably includes the other. The elevated buddhas of the universe, with their transcendent energy, are manifested in many different ways among us. If you exclude the external contrived forms, the spark of truth abounds in the tolling bells of a monastery at dawn, through the deep hum of a melodic organ, in the lamps and prayer flags of the Tibetan highlands, in gothic cathedrals, deep in Himalayan caves of the yogis, in the voyages of wanderers, in the chants of believers in saffron robes, in the hearts of denim-clad youth, in all the world's languages and dialects, in the silent flow of streams and rivers.

Free from a mentality of separation, putting forth boundless light, the awakened ones continue to work in their mysterious ways to transform sentient beings. Such workings are not graspable by refined language or specialized terminology. On a certain level, overemphasis on words and logic only creates distance from Truth, to the point of losing it altogether. "Mother" in English and *"mama"* in Chinese are essentially the same, yet expressed in different language symbols. If we rely on the truth beyond expression, we may find ourselves free of unnecessary verbal disputes.

I am also not a transmitter of the tantric tradition. Although my affiliation with Grandma has exposed me to many aspects of Tibetan Buddhism, and I have indeed gained spiritual rewards from such esoteric practices, these rewards were instrumental for nurturing the bodhi-seed within me, and were not intended to create delusions or confusion for persons who have wishful fantasies of spiritual gain. On this point, I am highly vigilant.

I subscribe to the notion that right faith does not rely on miracles. I believe, frankly, the biggest miracle is not to be angered when you have been insulted, and not to be intoxicated by praise. I know of people who keep their attainments hidden, who would rather contribute to others in secret, and avoid stirring up notoriety for themselves. I am a person who was enticed, step-by-step, aboard the Dharma-ship of the buddhas, and was given many lessons about fearless giving. I must continue to learn on this path, and not create confusion for others.

It is important not to take the attitude of the frog living at the bottom of a well, who believes its little glimpse is the entire sky, and points at clouds that float by, saying: "That is a supernatural phenomenon...you must be careful..."

Indeed, the cultivation of tantric practices can lead one to experience something "supernatural." Perhaps this is the reason many people approach it with enthusiasm. Aside from this, people in their weakness are no longer satisfied with the ideal of "self-reliant awakening." Tantra stresses that they should face life's deepest-rooted afflictions directly, and sublimate them to a transcendent level. It enables them to excavate meaning from our daily lives, and with its emphasis on empowerment and spiritual rewards, it provides a haven for our vulnerable hearts.

If one approaches tantric cultivation with ulterior motives, he will surely descend into lower paths of transmigration. What is more, attainment in tantric practices is not the true aim of Vajrayana, because under some circumstances, occult practices may turn out to be useless. Within the universe's great interwoven field of energy, facing the silence of underlying reality, in the eyes of Heaven and the buddhas, any type of contrived action or ritual is just an elaborate performance, neither esoteric nor exoteric in substance.

Tantra as I understand it is not a matter of beating drums, ringing bells and chanting scriptures, nor is it simply praying to end disasters and bring blessings. Rather, it is an invisible sword that has cut through my attachment to fame and material rewards; it has cut through my reliance on external things. This teaching has left me alone, stripped naked to face questions of gain and loss, form and formlessness, living and dying. The unremitting challenges therein were for me alone to experience. Such has been the effect of tantric teachings on me. I do not think many people will be interested in this type of esotericism. I seem to occupy a rather cold corner in today's colorful and multifaceted spiritual marketplace. In spite of that, however, I will never be lost in the wilderness, will not lose perspective, and will not turn toward sensationalism. This stability is something else that my tantric studies have given me.

The tantric path has given me an understanding of the Middle View[36]—a realization of the inherent emptiness that underlies colors and forms. Most importantly, my tantric studies have enabled me to transcend any religious affiliation, including the Vajrayana School itself.

Who am I, really, then? Within the infinite game of the universe, what role do I play? First, I am the granddaughter of Yeshe Tsuomu—she is a great master. She has shown me many true visions of Heaven and the human world, to further my life of wisdom in the Dharma-body.

There was a time that I was a working mother and wife. Due to certain circumstances, my husband left me, and my daughter left this world. What remains to me is the infinite expansion of motherly love.

I used to be a noted director, and have completed projects such as *China's Religious Cultures*, *Stories of the Tibetan Monks*, and numerous environmental film documentaries.

I have crossed China's mountains and rivers in search of enlightened masters, and have sat in the pews of Western churches to hear the transmission of Truth. Ultimately, I found that the road to awakening rests at every person's feet.

Due to karmic conditions, I was born and raised in Beijing, China, but was directed to come to America. While in Beijing, I served as a communicator within its highest governmental media agency; in America, I am a communicator of the highest truth—I have been designated as a transmitter. At the same time, I am a pragmatic doer. My specific calling to come to America draws on all the abilities I

---

36 The mind that transcends dualistic time-space categories gains insight into the substance behind phenomena. It is a balanced, impartial mind, thus is called the "Middle View" or Madhyamika.

possess, both by "nature" and "nurture." In Chapter 22, "A Great Prophecy," I have discussed this in greater detail.

I am a sentient being who seeks to evolve. The allures of worldly pursuits no longer hold any attraction for me—I am an objective observer, an outsider if you will, who watches flowers bloom and wither with detachment. The realm of impermanence is my playground.

Most importantly, I am an ordinary mortal. So ordinary, in fact, that I don't have any feeling of accomplishment or achievement. I have no such feelings now, but perhaps I shall in the future—at my moment of leaving earthly life I will joyously sing: "At last I return to my home in the light!"

I am a daughter of Heaven and earth, a real person outside the parameters of religious affiliation, without title or label. Although I am getting more advanced in years, my heart is becoming simpler. I speak the truth without reservation like a child, and seek to do real things without building a façade. If my words and conduct offer people any revelation and help, I must first acknowledge all the teachers and masters, the people and circumstances that have enabled and purified me.

Within the vast interplay of time and space and the realms beyond it, I am a person who has traveled from the East to the West at the turn of a new century. People may learn about me through a media source, or come across a woman pushing a shopping cart at the store, or encounter a woman stopped by the police due to a traffic violation. At another moment they may come across someone who sometimes gathers stones at the beach, or silently rests atop a mountain—*that is who I am.*

– PART II –

PHOENIX RISING

— 24 —

About Yoga of Joy

Traditions of yoga can be broadly divided into phenomenal and non-phenomenal yoga. Orthodox Vajrayana doctrine holds that phenomenal yoga is derived from mandala visualizations that align one's body, mind, and speech with the original master, thus arriving at "buddhahood within this body." Building upon phenomenal practice, non-phenomenal yoga contemplates inwardly and enters empty-naturedness to enable a higher realization. Vajrayana believes that the combination of phenomenal and non- phenomenal yoga can lengthen one's lifespan while advancing spiritually. Practice of phenomenal yoga alone, however, only serves to adjust bodily functions and cure illness.

Because Yoga of Joy has its roots in the Vajrayana tradition, it inevitably contains many tantric principles. But since it has been stripped of elaborate ritualistic forms, it is a practice that anyone can follow.

There are phenomenal and non-phenomenal aspects in Yoga of Joy also. The phenomenal part is the nine postures and the movements themselves. The non-phenomenal part is growth of awareness and understanding beyond the nine postures.

Through the regulation of the four elements of earth (skeleton), water (the bodily fluids and blood), fire (temperature), and wind (breath), one's internal feng shui is enhanced, resulting in refinement of the coarse, and a healthy body resistant to sickness.

Growth of awareness and knowledge causes one's inner capacity to expand. In that process, one's access to vast latent energy is released and elevated, enabling one to be victorious over negative emotions. Actually, reading this book can be a process of cultivating non-phenomenal yoga.

Yoga of Joy requires dual cultivation of the phenomenal with the non-phenomenal. One without the other would render the practice incomplete. The Chinese have a saying that "the body is the vessel of wisdom, and the home for nurturing virtue." To save someone who has fallen into the water, it is necessary to grab him by his clothing and pull him ashore. To take this analogy further, suppose that the person is the spirit, and the clothing is one's body. Through caring for our bodies, our spirits find release, and conversely, spiritual well-being leads to balanced bodily functions. Synergistic application of the spiritual and the material is a special attribute of Yoga of Joy.

There are many yoga teachers in America—some of them are great practitioners who have attained wisdom through spiritual practice. Others, however, have grouped the practice of yoga with general calisthenics and gymnastics. We all have seen yoga teachers with beautifully sculpted bodies who are able to perform amazing physical feats with grace. When I was teaching at the Philosophical Research Society, some of my students asked me what the difference is between

Yoga of Joy, and the traditional yoga seen in the West. My answer was that yoga teachers in the West are wonderful people, but some of them give only a beautiful vase to their students, without any flowers in it. Yoga of Joy has not only the beautiful vase, but it also contains the flowers. The smiles I get from this response tell me that people are beginning to understand the real calling of a yoga practice.

The non-phenomenal part of Yoga of Joy penetrates the pain of living and identifies the cause of suffering. Penetrating awareness of suffering is not supposed to fill us with angst; rather, it gives us illumination to cut through the cause of suffering once and for all. Through elevation of one's spirit, Yoga of Joy allows one to see through the illusory masks this world puts on, and connect with the essential nature of the universe. But this takes deeply rooted wisdom.

What is our awareness to penetrate, and how?

Of All Awareness, the Most Valuable Is Awareness of Mortality

Being born as a human is indeed a gift, because it offers a certain freedom. But the price of this precious chance is accepting death's inevitability. Regardless of whether one is a king or beggar, we are all equal before death. What mock us are the unpredictable time of death, and the fleeting impermanent nature of happiness. The richest person cannot take a single item with him at the time of death. When a person faces death, he does so nakedly, hungrily, and without any props to his dignity. In the face of death, it makes no difference whether a king leaves behind a kingdom or a beggar leaves behind his begging bowl. In our daily life, we face all kinds of hardships and difficulties.

Living as we do in the age of the Dharma's decline, we are faced with many distractions that make it hard to commit to a rigorous spiritual practice.

It matters not how high our status is, or whether we hail from East or West, none of us are granted immunity from pain and suffering. Every one of us, if we quietly observe our worries and pain will conclude that things of this world are like a mirage or dream, without power in themselves to give us happiness. Everyone wishes for blessings, looks forward to happiness, and longs for release from suffering and pain. If this longing grows stronger, we eventually need to awaken by probing directly into death and suffering. If we avoid this we are deceiving ourselves. In Chinese Buddhism we have a saying: Of all right-minded contemplations, illumination of death is most valuable.

In our lifetimes, from the time that we can remember, we have encountered suffering and difficulties that are beyond our control. Things we cannot change are lining up, one after another, over time. At the end of the line comes the biggest inevitability of all, which is death. Against this inevitability, all other challenges pale in comparison. Thus, I wish to persuade those who find themselves perpetually wallowing among the smaller inevitabilities to resolve the largest one first. At the very least, this will serve to elevate their wisdom-energy.

What happens after we die, and what happens in the afterlife, are things we cannot foretell. Attachment to materialistic illusions causes many obstacles to arise between oneself and a serious commitment to spiritual cultivation. Yet by virtue of inherent Dharma-nature, human beings have the chance to realize the goal of evolving to higher planes of existence.

The True Energy Source

Christians call this era the "end times," and for the Buddhists, it is the "decline of the Dharma." During this time, all sentient beings live in disharmony and pain. The suffering of mortal enemies can bring no consolation. In the 21st Century there will be more people with mental illnesses. The poor have one type of heartache and the rich have another. Each person becomes the bearer of his own sorrowful story. As sorrow spreads from person to person, it differs only in specifics.

Even professional psychoanalysts and psychologists have severe mental traumas and abnormalities. In such a setting, it is no wonder that many have enthusiasm for activities that replenish "energy." What is this energy that people are seeking? Is it the beauty of youthful features, or is it wealth that we cannot take with us? Is it the intoxication of love, or is it the edgy thrill of being in the spotlight? These forms of energy that many people rave over are no match for natural laws. Therefore, wisdom teaches living things to enjoy a different kind of "hedonism." First of all we need to change our understanding of "energy." Western research in holistic medicine points to a force not measurable in crude physical terms called *bio-energy*.

Energy can indeed be stored in our spiritual bodies, existing in a form more subtle than micro-particles. This energy source does not rely on vitamins. It is not sexual attraction, nor is it the stimulus of material gain. There is no material measure of its components. It is only gained through inner cultivation that attunes one's heart and mind to the universal frequency of the divine. Modern science has proven that emotional states such as anger, grief, and joy can cause immediate chemical changes at the cellular level, leading to production of harmful or beneficial substances. The overall effect of yogic practice is to let *prajna* (wisdom) grow out of *samadhi* (absorption), at the same time tapping latent sources to raise one's mind-body energy level. By aligning with the frequency of universal energy, one can arrive at an optimal energy state.

The human body at the cellular level replaces itself completely once every seven years. This can be called a kind of reincarnation in the present lifetime. Living those seven years in pain and worry only causes our current incarnation to age and deteriorate prematurely. Thus the truly wise will understand and use this natural cycle, becoming acquainted with subtle energy to replenish it properly. This is "hedonism" that is truly worth pursuing—the "hedonism" of good health.

Yoga and Energy

What is the ultimate purpose of life, and what are worthwhile goals? Where do we come from, and where are we going? What do the laws of the universe mean for the course of human development? To understand these questions, the sages of the past have developed a technique, and that is yoga.

The original meaning of "yoga" is "union" or "alignment". Through yogic practice, the human spirit can resonate with universal Truth. With such an alignment, man is then able to leave suffering and find joy. This is the calling and aspiration of yoga. What it gives to human beings is the most precious form of energy that exists.

Many sages and teachers throughout history have told us, by virtue of their own experience, what is beneficial and what is injurious for human beings. We know that everyone desires happiness and wishes to avoid pain and suffering. This desire extends itself through time, toiling its way through lifetime after lifetime. But so often people are reduced to a desperate plight by pursuit of their own desires. This happens because they fail to keep one thing in mind: in order to have ultimate happiness and avoid sorrow from lifetime to lifetime, it is necessary to identify one's nemesis—the five poisons. The five poisons in the Buddhist tradition are the afflictions of Grasping, Resentment, Delusion, Arrogance, and Doubt.

Grasping causes a heated, restless state; we become perturbed over what we cannot possess, which makes our facial features detestable. Resentment strains the nervous and endocrine systems, disrupts internal secretions, damages the liver, and threatens our sanity. Delusion makes us believe the superficial appearance of things, supposing they exist in and of themselves, without reliance on conditions. Delusion is the source of perversity and causes people to be prideful, partial and selfish. The resulting narrow-mindedness and suspicion makes it hard to believe in Truth.

Selfishness is a major reason for the predicaments people find themselves in. We look out for ourselves, and so often neglect others. A selfish attitude is like a thief that has arrived in our hearts. He carries with him a bag filled with desire, resentment and delusion, and takes away our good nature and compassion. We are each responsible for our losses and failures, and our suffering is derived from fixation on our own well-being. So we have to learn to care about others, to de-emphasize our lesser self and make room for our larger self. The inner poise and serenity we find will keep us from being thrown off balance by outside circumstances. Our bodies in themselves become a blissful ground, no longer prey to inner conflict or outer trauma.

Our bodies and minds together will then constitute a "peace zone." When one's cultivation reaches this stage, every act and utterance fit into the yoga of joy.

In my many personal trials and tribulations, I too have been threatened by negative emotions. But as I continually get more familiar with my larger, cosmically grounded self, I feel its presence enfolding me more closely. One characteristic of the heart-mind is that the closer we get to the object of our feelings, the more familiar we are with it, then the more stable our relationship with it becomes. Qualities of mind and spirit know no limits, unlike our body with its limitations. Our heart is like a fire: the more fuel we give it, the brighter it burns.

The fuel that our heart draws on is our wish for liberation. It is an honest and sincere desire to receive the truth; it is the strength of devotion and perseverance in faith.

Undoubtedly, our afflictions are a strong and tricky foe, which cannot be tamed without the power of wisdom. Whatever kind of ignorance we deal with, it cannot withstand the test of wisdom; the worst afflictions collapse under wisdom's penetrating gaze. Only wisdom can fully eradicate afflictions, for its essence is compassion. If we accept this we will have faith, and the numerous problems afflicting us transform into "karmic opportunities"— helping us find liberation and open the luminous world of self-nature.

Motives for Self-Cultivation

Prior to our study of Yoga of Joy, we need to get our motivation straight. The purpose of our practice is neither to please anyone else nor to satisfy a thirst for novelty. It stems from our responsible concern over our own suffering and happiness. In the final analysis, what shall we choose? Shall we possess joy, or shall we be entangled in mundane suffering? Indeed the future of mankind actually rests in our own hands. These are the fundamental motives to practice Yoga of Joy.

With this type of motivation, the practice of Yoga of Joy becomes a life-decision based in wisdom. It can ensure our bodily and mental wholeness. And with perseverance it will provide you with more than a healthy body, it will transmute your attitudes and let your heart grow gracefully.

Any type of cultivation begins with the spirit. Mindfulness is cultivated so we can master our restless, confused nature, and to sweep our spirits clear of ignorance and attachment. Yogic practice is intended to sweep away affliction just as rays of sunlight dispel darkness. Thus many yogis are called gurus for their ability to dispel darkness.

An interval when Yoga of Joy is practiced is a serene, deeply immersed moment. It is also a time full of feelings. The feelings that come out are expressions of spirit—sympathy for the poor and sick, compassion for our enemies. Obviously it is a challenge to show such composure when confronted with real-life pain and suffering. In this regard, our yogic practice is not an act, nor is it separated from everyday life. It is training for real life, not a costume that we put on and take off.

The practitioner should not restrict himself to certain times and places in seeking yogic awareness. He fills the days of his life with pure and benevolent intent, keeping mind and body in harmony. Anyone who can tap into his life-affirming, upright qualities is a true yoga practitioner; this is not measured by how many difficult postures one can execute beautifully. Our sincerity and good-heartedness, as seen in our bearing and behavior, are expressions of our yoga.

Mental Acclimation

The place of practice should be clean, airy and quiet. As you clean your place of practice, however, visualize that the place that most needs cleaning is one's own heart and spirit.

As you practice Yoga of Joy, your heart must be sincere and respectful. If you make Truth your master at every moment, there will be joy and reverence in your heart. Pray often to the master for guidance, and frequently reflect upon your own mistakes. If you can do this, then whether you meet with happy or sad occasions, whether you receive praise or scorn, as all manner of adversities and opportunities rush toward you, you will never doubt the existence of Truth. Divine blessings are to be sought in reverence, working from the ground up, making slow and steady advances, until one day we see the effects for ourselves. That is when we will prove the benefits of Yoga of Joy in the most direct and personal manner.

If you really wish to solidify the effects of this yoga, you must not be like the fisherman who fishes two days, then hangs up his net for seven. Otherwise, you will lose the effect of all your prior efforts. By applying yourself day after day, month after month, year after year, you will find that "Heaven rewards the diligent." When that day comes, you will see how attractive you can be, both in inner qualities and outer appearance. Since coming to America, I have met many "spiritual shoppers" who are constantly running from guru to teacher, spending time and energy making selections and rankings. They lack the requisite seriousness and sincerity in their quest, and sadly, they themselves lose the most ultimately: they have treated their own spirituality as a leisure pursuit.

Although the ultimate aim of Yoga of Joy is to depart from pain and find joy, one's state during practice should be to let go of joy, sorrow, or any sort of "doing" whatsoever. To be successful, one must be willing to endure loneliness. The practice of yoga is not in essence a noisy group activity, nor does it rely on external aids. The ideal state is an inward, reflective, peaceful attitude. In the course of practice, it is common for emotions to arise—be they negative reactions to the spiritual adjustment taking place, or other natural outpourings. One must persevere through these common reactions until the practice stabilizes. This is when spiritual joy will emerge—a special joy that is unattached and needs no occasioning circumstances.

A Meaningful Mental Adjustment

The practitioner of Yoga of Joy also needs to understand how to "unite with Heaven and meld with life itself." It is important to view all that happens in life, good or bad, happy or sad, victory or failure, with the right understanding. Nothing is absolutely black or white in life, since things come in colors, and the degree of illumination changes.

When looked at from a negative angle, misfortunes naturally lead to pain and depression. From another vantage point, however, if you compare your hardships with someone less fortunate, you will actually feel rather lucky. If you choose to view your experience in this manner, you will come to a deeper understanding of the relative nature of suffering, and be able to deal with your life in a more accepting, relaxed and open manner. But if you cannot adjust your own perspective, you will have unlimited reasons to be unhappy and depressed.

In order to create joy in one's life, the role of mind and spirit must be emphasized. In fact, the best adjustment can be made by contemplating the paths taken by great saints and sages: Sakyamuni Buddha left his earthly kingdom to pursue higher wisdom and Christ was nailed on the cross, all to release living beings from suffering. People often admire their greatness, but forget the pain they endured on the road to enlightenment.

The practice of Yoga of Joy also encourages us to make offerings in spirit to harmful forces. We should ponder the gifts we receive from the "enemy." A very accomplished yogi once made this prayer: "Your continuous persecution enabled me to strengthen my practice; the pain you caused has elevated my compassion and patience. You have given me an extraordinary chance to be tested. Please, continue in your persecutions!" Is this not an evolved, humorous wisdom, turning what is considered hurtful into empowerment? Yield one step to get more breathing room; yield ten steps to walk with the sages.

Yoga of Joy is based upon values that are not materialistic. It calls on the practitioner to see giving and receiving from a spiritual perspective. There is an old saying: "He who exceeds his earthly share will suffer loss in Heaven." Do not be tainted by acquisitive motives, but always seek to galvanize yourself in body, speech and mind, to devote your resources to creating well-being for others. This kind of sacrifice will be recorded in your subtle spirit-body, bringing you even greater rewards. Remember that you can take nothing with you when you die except the karma you have accumulated for yourself. Grandma used to say to me: "If you borrow from your field of blessings to plant someone else's, you will be repaid a thousand-fold." Heaven treats us fairly and never miscalculates. But if we think of what we stand to receive, this is not giving. To give with one hand while taking with the other is inauthentic and ineffective.

Recover Lost Innocence and Joy

The cultivation of Yoga of Joy is a return to pure innocence, a restoration of youth. In one sense, it is the best type of beauty makeover. Purity refers to pure knowing and seeing. Youth means finding our natural ageless and innocent state. Once we are reacquainted with our primordial openness, fearlessness and peace, those traces of our old selves that mar our faces will be gone.

The "joy" in Yoga of Joy requires a deep process of integral cultivation. My trials in samsara have taught me there are many connotations to the word "joy." But the highest, truest joy is prajna wisdom. This is wisdom that turns the world into Heaven.

To help us arrive at wisdom, even the names of Joyful Yoga's nine steps have an elevating, guiding effect. You can even say that the name of each posture is a mantra in itself. The names are: *Between Heaven and Earth, Snow Lotus in the Mountains, Childhood Days, Always Smiling, Sword of Wisdom, Pyramid Constellation, Oasis in the Desert, Yeshe Tsuomu (Ocean of Wisdom),* and *Return to Nature.* Each title embraces a certain state for contemplating and receiving guidance. In doing so, you will be able to access the elevated personal energy behind this yoga.

Mindful readers who feel a connection may want to know more about this "personal energy." Because this practice is a transmitted teaching with its own particular origin and heritage, it naturally has its own energy source. Therefore when you practice it, try not to judge it against other yogic practices. Although some of the physical postures may resemble other "asanas," they are qualitatively different in terms of the spiritual energy at work. The names of the postures point to body-mudras and postures that guide the flow of energy in accordance with right contemplation. Ultimately, you will experience the deeper meanings of the postures through your own practice.

I will cite one instance that tells us something of the power behind Yoga of Joy. In June of 2000, I went to a party with one of my students who had only practiced Yoga of Joy three times. At the party we met an Englishwoman named Linda, who had followed a spiritual path in India for over twenty years, and is now a well-known psychic with followers of her own. Someone wanted to see what Yoga of Joy was, so I asked my student to demonstrate. After watching quietly from the side while my student performed three of the postures, Linda said that the light given off by this practice was among the fastest and strongest of any she had seen. Being a cautious person, Linda asked the student to repeat the postures. After watching a second time, she declared that this technique indeed generated light more quickly than any she had seen.

In this book, I have chosen to focus closer attention on the Ninth Step, which is called *Return to True Nature*.

— 25 —

Return to True Nature

Dumu is a Tibetan word, which in Sanskrit is known as *Candali-yoga*, and means "strong light". According to the *Supreme Tantric Yoga Sutra,* there are four types of Dumu luminosity: External, Internal, Secret, and Empty-Natured. The External luminosity subjugates demons; the Internal luminosity regulates the four elements of earth, water, fire and wind; the Secret luminosity breaks down 84,000 kinds of afflictions; and the Empty-Natured luminosity gives insight into true self-nature.

Realization through Dumu can cause a person to give rise to supreme happiness or ecstasy, and thereby enter into a Samadhi of luminous awareness.

Types of Transmission

One kind of a transmission of Dumu is through observances such as those described in *The Practice of the Six Yogas of Naropa,* which is fitting for monastics, especially lamas. This kind of transmission requires that a person visualize the chi, the central channel and the luminescent points within it, mainly from a seated posture. It emphasizes spiritual heat—probably because in the snowy high plateau, the weather is very cold, and through this "heat" one can assess the results of this practice. But the energy of Dumu is far greater than just melting ice and keeping warm.

Another means of transmission is the dakini transmission, which does not fall into any religious framework; rather it manifests form in empty-naturedness. What I transmit is this second kind of transmission. This method is fairly intuitive and simple, and it's used for people who have a spiritual nature but are not constrained by any particular religion and have the power of their strong commitment. This second kind is Vajra Yoga Dakini transmission. It is more like the dance of Shiva, which integrates the dancer with the myriad forms of the cosmos. It is also called Kundalini Shakti. Kundalini is the dragon of awakening; Shakti is the phoenix of rebirth from fire. Dumu awakening is the practical method of dragon-flying and phoenix-dancing to attain great self-realization.

Beginning: The Four Levels of Life

The first level is the physical body, which is the gross body, formed out of earth, water, fire and wind. Earth symbolizes the bodily frame, water symbolizes bodily fluids, fire is bodily heat, and wind is the breath. When these four elements are out of tune the person falls ill; when they disperse, the person dies.

The second level is the emotional body. The emotions can be an important driving force, but the push and pull among them creates conditions for aging, episodes of illness and mishaps. Even a good person who cannot control his or her moods may often commit foolish acts. They may hurt others or do injury to themselves, and may even commit suicide. If someone gives free rein to anger or to their habitual series of moods, letting them play across their face, it shows that they are superficial and immature. It is therefore important to stabilize the emotional body.

The third level is the heart/mind wisdom body, which includes consciousness, rationality, and conceptual thought. It is more subtle than the emotional body, yet it contains many unnatural pollutants such as delusions, grasping, anger, pride and suspicion. This can be an arena of conflict, creating discord and trouble.

The fourth level is the heavenly body. Its fineness is distributed through 72,000 meridians, the seven chakras, as well as in *chi*, the central channel, and luminescent points. The heavenly body is an energy field that is associated with the untapped 90% of human potential. When activated, it provides powerful spirit-energy. When tapped into it feels like flowing with waves, moving along with air currents, or like a consuming fire. Not only does this act to harmonize mind and body, it has extraordinary powers that escort us "back home". The tapping-into process I speak of is the activation of Dumu energy; the home I speak of is our innate radiant self-nature.

Activating the Dumu Energy

There are four methods for activating the Dumu energy: aside from using the eyes to transmit, hands to touch and mind to impart, the most often-used method is to use mantric singing to activate the source of light. This is a method within supreme yoga, where a master transmits or activates Dumu in another. The mind power of both the activator and recipient are important in this process. Between them there needs to be openness; they must trust each other. The recipient must not be doubtful or critical, and even a fond mental state would be out of place. In Vajra Buddhism, the activation of Dumu is called a tantric empowerment. An important factor in this is the recipient's level of realization. This is because the high masters of the universe shine their light impartially, like the sun shines everywhere in the human world. However, obstructions cause some areas to be overcast. This is not the fault of the sun; the obstruction itself is the cause. Thus, empowerment needs two-way interaction. In Chinese, the word "empowerment" means, "impart and hold". If something is imparted to someone, it is up to the recipient to "hold" it to use for self-cultivation.

A very few people have the activation occur on their own without conscious intention, and they might think this energy is negative or dangerous. If this is the case, it's necessary to establish a sense of security. I would like to introduce a great protector called Pure Clear Mind, which if adopted, will ensure the safety and protection of the practitioner. Please remember that all phenomena are only games of the mind, and if one always uses the clear, pure mind to look into things, then there will be no cause for alarm.

Putting the Radiant Heart in Charge

The ultimate result of Dumu energy's wisdom is to burn away ignorance in mind and body, to let self-nature flush out slavish dependencies, to let it achieve great release, great suppleness and perfect poise. Therefore the experience of the Dumu energy is only a facilitator: the eventual goal is to elevate this energy into the light of awakening, to put the Radiant Heart in charge.

This process lets the practitioner break loose from all concepts and all religious formalism, to enable him or her to directly rejoin the Source of Nature. Instead of chasing about outwardly, it allows a direct resonance with all things from within oneself; it is growing out of the limited self into the boundless Infinite Self. It is Zen. It is Tantra. It is the supreme all-nurturing water of Lao Tzu. It is the Spirit Dragon of Heaven. It is the Ascending Phoenix, wherein the weak changes into the strong, pain changes into joy, and ignorance changes into wisdom. It is also God and the practitioner abiding as one—thus the Dumu experience is beyond religion.

Reactions to the Dumu Energy

The characteristic nature of Dumu energy is an inward-seeking of roots as well as in an outward expansion. The Dumu energy is an intelligent energy that automatically and spontaneously seeks out any impurities, and it then purifies and clears them. It has an ultra-sensitive ability to stay on track and regulate itself. It honestly reckons with the Tao of the human body, never in a contrived manner. Often its real cleansing work begins from the coarser levels. It is like an intelligent washing machine designed by an advanced cosmic intelligence. It knows clearly what steps to take; it knows which clothes need hard scrubbing and which need gentle washing. The entire process comes from the great order of Nature itself.

The process of awakening Dumu will often bring on reactions, such as:

Reactions of the Physical Body

Upon activating the Dumu energy, one initially feels charged up with energy. This may be a feeling of warmth, coolness, swelling, numbness, etc. The energy is quite powerful when it begins operating, exerting a pull that causes one to sway, to spin in circles, to walk backwards, to run and jump, or to raise arms or legs in the air. It may, for example, compel the practitioner to lie down and roll on the ground due to the presence of environmental pollutants in the body that can cause illnesses; in this case the contact with the earth element will dispel them.

Another example is of a person who suffered from a neck ailment. Following activation, he was induced to make neck-swiveling movements that would normally have been difficult. With the help of Dumu, he felt no particular pain and continued the swiveling until one day he no longer felt the urge to make the movements, and found that he was fully recovered from his long-term neck ailment. Next, the Dumu energy led him to make a new movement: his right hand began to pat his chest with a sustained forceful motion. This would normally have made him uneasy, but while patting in the Dumu state he felt relaxed and at ease. After performing this practice for a period of time he was examined by a doctor, who told him, "Your coronary arteries have cleared up, so you won't need medication anymore!"

A few people, after activation, feel quite uncomfortable. During the body movement, they might feel anxious, have a headache or experience some other symptom. They might think, "I'm supposed to feel very comfortable, very good. Why do I feel sick?" Feeling unwell is normal, because some current or possibly older hidden sickness is coming out to be cleansed. The anxiousness, headache, nausea or uncomfortable feeling is just the process of removing toxins.

These physical symptoms are like blessings in disguise, because after the feeling of sickness passes the practitioner is given the opportunity to encounter their natural self without illness. In addition, the integrating energy of Dumu also affects and may alter the senses, potentially reflected in sleep, eating and drinking habits, and the sense of smell. For instance, someone who previously was unable to eat cold food may now want to eat ice cream, someone who loved to eat meat may suddenly be interested in becoming a vegetarian, or someone who has had a preference for one kind of fruit may change to a different food.

Reactions of the Emotional Body

After Dumu is activated, various emotions will emerge. This is a way of expelling or releasing them to attain balance. Dumu can dissolve the deep-level negative emotions such as moods that have burdened the practitioner for a long time, perhaps even from a previous lifetime. Negative emotions are a "sinking" energy of the densest kind, so they can lead to bodily illness. As they come to the surface, one's true self needs to rise above and look upon the experience as an observer, and while watching, be mindful not to succumb to the emotional states as they pass through consciousness.

Reactions of the Heart/Mind Wisdom Body

Following activation of the Dumu energy, the mental formation gradually shifts from a controlling to an observing perspective. It watches its own body being adjusted and cured by a deeper, stronger energy. This has a challenging, dissipating effect on tense, mechanical thought patterns that insist on doing things a certain way. Questions arise, such as, "What is that innate presence?" "How expansive is its domain?" "Aside from tuning and curing the body, does it have other areas of potential?"

Perhaps the practitioner might see supernatural light, a blue pearl, or various spatial realms. Perhaps there will be unusual feelings in the third-eye chakra, crown chakra, throat chakra or heart chakra. He or she might emit sounds without intending to. If this was to occur, the directive is not to be nervous, but to simply allow the natural course. Whatever is experienced is normal. Because we live in a world that is in fact multi-dimensional, this is nothing more than the spiritual eye awakening from sleep and disclosing the underlying reality. Another possibility may be a change in dream life, with some remarkable new experiences in dreams.

It is even more intriguing that people who have never learned yogic or tai-chi movements may be impelled by the Dumu energy to perform them, or perhaps perform a ritual dance, such as the 108 dance steps of Shiva. All of these movements allow the heart/mind wisdom to slip free from the limits of three-dimensional space in a dualistic world. They are also to familiarize the practitioner with "empty consciousness" in order to allow an opening for awareness of a higher order.

A reaction by the heart/mind wisdom body might be that a person who has never healed others may suddenly have healing energy and the ability to help others, or may suddenly have an intuition of future events. They may feel that spiritual powers are beckoning them. The practitioner must be aware and honest with him/herself and remember their true "beginning" level in order to prevent arrogance, which would bring them harm.

Another reaction by the mental formation is quite interesting. People who are normally self-satisfied and opinionated have a hard time believing in something sincerely. But without realizing it, when the Dumu energy is activated, they may kneel on the ground and pray; they may pray and repent for some time. The light of Dumu is working to remedy their heart's limited views and bring out something beyond the mental level.

The Dumu may also make possible a "replay" of something from a person's past that is stored in their subconscious. While going through this process, the practitioner must dare to put down all attachments until nothing at all is left; for it is then that the everyday mind is most open to the experience. Without expectation, without premeditation, without analysis, without imitation, the practitioner rests at the unmoving center. This state allows the real self to clearly observe the self that is in illusion, and through consistent practice use the illusory to cultivate the real truth.

Without taking aim, the practitioner will hit the bull's eye of their potential; discriminating consciousness will transform to wisdom in a quantum leap.

> *Outside of Goals,*
> *Attaining the Great Goal,*
> *Outside of Rules,*
> *Fitting in with the Great Rule.*

This is a realm of emptiness, and only when you reach this will you be able to bring forth pure Dumu. Only in this way can the ultimate miracle happen – without beginning and without end, you return to the universal wellspring. It sure is nice to "come home"!

Though countless wonders beckon, do not prolong your stay; do not forget to return.

Right Practice

People may ask, "How long will it take until I reach this marvelous level?" Empirical evidence has proven that it is determined by the individual. Under conditions of right thought, right faith and right effort, as long as you can renounce bad habit patterns or let them dissipate, then karma will dissolve at that moment and your journey will have a perfect beginning.

Under certain conditions of affinity, you can even transform calamity into opportunity. But this does not mean that you have been granted immunity from suffering. It is important to build up your capacity for joy, so that in the face of hardship and suffering, you can remain poised and grateful, composed and serene. This is the blessing that Dumu awakens.

In Dumu training, the biggest taboos are racking your brain to imitate some pattern, or being in a hurry to achieve something. What is to be avoided is making contrived, obsessive attempts to achieve this Return to True Nature. Any kind of advantage-seeking or impatience for success is strictly ruled out. If you fall victim to aberrant physical or mental behavior, or engage in self-promotion or financially profit from the use of paranormal powers, you may call retribution down on yourself. This would be wholly due to your violation of the spiritual principles involved—a fruit of indulgence in wrong thinking. People are harmed by their own clever tricks. What is advocated is this:

> *Make vows without attachment,*
> *Expend effort without insistence,*
> *Cherish without being stuck,*
> *Rejoice without keeping score.*

— 26 —

Baja Elements

I grew up in a rural environment (our Agricultural College was like a village). Later I worked for the Central Television programs Homeland Attractions and Man in Nature, which gave me chances to visit spectacular mountains and rivers. Both in Beijing and in America I have lived in prime scenic areas. Although I did not set out to be picky, it was as if I had been "chosen" by those favorable spots to live in pristine surroundings.

Once I lived in seclusion awhile in a place called Baja. Baja is a peninsula with many islands in Mexico. There is a volcano there, and desert terrain where many kinds of cactus grow. The area where I stayed is frequented by Americans, who can easily reach it by car or private plane. Northern Baja Bay is a special place where warm waters of the Colorado River used to empty into the Pacific, and in doing so, created a fertile maritime ecosystem. The Sea of Cortes is a gathering place for blue whales, humpback whales, dolphins and giant sharks. Other noteworthy places are Moon Valley and the nearby Indian village site. The hills overlooking Moon Valley consist of calcareous deposits from marine animals, which prove that the area was once on the ocean floor. At night, moonlight causes the chalk mountains to sparkle, as if stars had descended to the earth. Because this area is off the electrical grid, it preserves many features of a primitive environment. There is no noise but the engine sounds of speedboats or helicopters as they occasionally pass by.

The Baja Peninsula is sparsely populated, and in such a setting one seldom needs to speak, so your mouth can get a taste of quietness. There is no need to decipher speech, so your auditory faculty goes back to a pristine state. At such times I observe things with three kinds of eyes. My first pair of eyes can see traces of pythons, patterned scales of iguanas and birds riding wind currents in the sky; now and then they see a porpoise or whale breaching on the ocean surface. I have another pair of eyes—binoculars—which can bring these animals close enough to inspect their detailed features. My third kind of eye is the mind's eye, which goes beyond material things to gaze at my true home.

During the months of my spiritual retreat in Baja, what did I see in my "true home"? Two scenes remain especially fresh in my memory.

A white-garbed young woman poled a skiff along a winding stream that led to an ancient looking walled city. After disembarking she led me through a large door and motioned me to wait in a rear courtyard. I leaned against a high wall, craning my neck to see what was on the other side. I saw three old men in a circle, sitting cross-legged at the center of an open area. One of them was round-faced and beardless, but the other two were relatively slender and had long whiskers. They wore long robes of grayish-blue and all were immersed in samadhi. I walked into that open area, placing my feet gingerly to avoid making noise. Then I noticed that the open area was ringed by a large number of people whose eyes were closed and whose hands were positioned in mudras. I was absorbed in figuring out the mudras when the rotund old man walked over to me. He led me back to the open space and told me to sit facing the other two elders. But the two old men were in deep samadhi and seemed hidden from me. By the time I remembered what they looked like, I discovered that the rotund old man had gone away. I looked for him in all directions, and then looked down to find that I was standing on water, and the water was reflecting a golden light. I lifted my head to see the rotund old man, and his whole body was giving off beams of gold light. Towering over me in a stately pose, he looked at me with a compassionate smile. I fell down on my knees and called out "Master," beginning to sob. He laid his hand on my head for a moment, then said, "Go back now." So I came back.

The other vision happened like this… I returned to that grand courtyard, and again I entered through the "back door." I saw the three old men sitting in a small circle. This time instead of being in samadhi they were amusing themselves by doing mudras with their hands. They formed a succession of mudras so adeptly that rainbow-colored light began to shine from between their fingers. Suddenly a flying phoenix appeared amid the beams of light from their fingers. The phoenix was not large, but it had splendid colors. As the phoenix was flying in gyres through the air, the rotund old man turned to me as if to say, "Do you understand what you just saw?" In an instant I found myself back on an earthly landscape. There I saw a grand phoenix descending from the sky to alight on a mountain peak. Its long plumed tail merged into the afterglow of sunset. The phoenix extended its beautiful head across the landscape and serenely gazed at me, face to face.

For a long time I was absorbed in recalling these two visions. Whether I was viewing sunbeams through clouds with my bare eyes or spotting dolphins with binoculars, that phoenix image would keep floating up from the waters of my subconscious mind.

Whether in ancient countries from the Far East to the Middle East (China, India, Egypt) or in modern times, people have handed down legends of the phoenix. Every thousand years the phoenix consumes itself in its own flames, then rises again from its own ashes. Buddhists sometimes peak of "the nirvana of a phoenix," which refers to such an idea.

The 21st Century will be a time for the phoenix's rebirth. Various religions have begun to show some degree of aging. People call such aging the "end times" or the "age of Declining Dharma." However, the world never really passes through end times, and the dharma is neither born nor extinguished. What some call the "end times" is perhaps "reaching an extreme". As for the "Declining Dharma," this really signifies the death of human hearts. Everywhere you go in the world, you hear the word *mang* ("busy"). In Chinese characters, the word is composed of "heart" and "disappear/pass away". If one's heart passes away, isn't that the decline of the dharma? As for self-immolation of the heart-mind, that comes about due to the five poisons.[37] When people are reduced to ash by self-immolation, this is the "end times" or "reaching the extreme". When one is reborn from the ashes, this is renewal or "approaching peace".

---

37 Five poisons: attachment, anger, ignorance, pride, and doubt.

On the Wings of Phoenix Rising

Ascension of the phoenix requires prayer and belief and acts that make renewal happen. In individual terms, your loss and pain and blows you suffer may put your faith and love through a conflagration. Perhaps some of your "wherewithal" may escape disaster, or perhaps it will all be reduced to ashes. Thus you will be plunged into despair and helplessness and fury. Perhaps you will retreat into the "Gate of Emptiness," or a sense of futility will prey upon you. You may lose your beliefs and entertain thoughts of suicide, or you may devise all sorts of ways to maximize sensory pleasure, passing your days in a deluded fog. You may thirst to possess more, envying those who outdo you and disdaining those who cannot rival you. Your heart may be filled with fear—fear of illness, fear of aging, fear of death, fear of earthquakes, fear of poverty, fear of abandonment, fear of an airplane crash, fear of unsafe highways…all these high and low flames are licking away at your Buddha-mind.

Let the phoenix of our life-force be reborn from this heap of ashes! Even now "approaching peace" is gazing at you in the form of a lovely phoenix.

Early this year I went back to Baja. I picked up feathers that were shed by birds flying by; I picked up bits of seashell on the beach and I gathered desert plants. I put these together with tea leaves, Japanese *sumi-e* ink and Korean pigments. In a shakti-state of open receptivity, I let a phoenix's energy be transformed into these paintings. I hardly used an ink brush at all.

I hope that friends who view these paintings can resonate with blessings from the phoenix!

— 27 —

A Story about Hair

I was brought into this world by my grandma Yeshe Tsuomu. Not only did she give me the name Yuan Miao (resonant with the alchemy of water), she also instilled in me a strong interest in the intangible power of hair.

Grandma loved to sing songs, but I could not understand the words. After reaching adulthood I realized that her chants included invocations to the Five Taras of the Himalayas, to the river gods of the Yarlung watershed and to the elements of earth, water, fire, wind and void. While Grandma sang her mantric chants, she would amuse herself by braiding my hair. She would plait my hair into numerous tiny braids until they hung down in a fringe. She would grind up "fingernail herb" into a paste, and then daub it between my eyebrows, making me look like a girl fresh from a Tibetan district. These distinctive marks, along with my dark skin, made me instantly recognizable in our staff residential compound. Whenever I wanted to cut my hair short, Grandma would say that my long hair was good for covering up my "print," which was a red birthmark on the nape of my neck. According to Grandma, the significance of my mark would someday be recognized by an advanced adept. Years later when I came to America, my mark really did prove to be my means of being "verified."

Sometimes Grandma would braid her own hair. Even though her hair grew sparse, it was still long, and gleaming from the osmanthus oil she rubbed on it. Sometimes she would plait lots of small braids, singing and laughing like a young beauty. She would say, "When I braid your hair, it is *xiufa* for me. Do you know what *xiufa* means? It doesn't mean I'm working on my *fa* (hair); it means I'm working on *fa* as in *fofa* (dharma)." This teaching stayed with me as I sought insight into human life and traveled about transmitting joyous wisdom.

When I reached the age of eight or nine, the Cultural Revolution broke out, and my school closed down. Grandpa was hauled away to the countryside. When we weren't scheming to get juicy tomatoes and watermelons, my little brother and I were stirring up a ruckus. The large pair of scissors kept at home was clumsy and rusty, but I took infinite delight in trimming my brother's hair. I would start by cutting a single lock; then I would get into creative styling. His hairstyle attracted a group of our playmates, who lined up wanting a trim from me. None of these hairstyles was like any other, and the hair length was uneven, but I was delighted to do it. We would look at each other and explode into laughter… In the evening when our parents came back from a political study session, they heard a cry of dismay from Uncle He who lived next door, followed by his Cantonese accented exclamation: "What have you done? It looks like the child has been chewed by a dog." That evening two of the parents came to our house with their bedraggled children in tow, complaining to my father and mother. For the next few days I was grounded. Perhaps because of the scolding I got that day, the world has been deprived of a great hairstylist.

As I matured I acquired two nicknames—"Long Legs" and "Long Braids." During my basketball-playing years, those flailing braids were a distraction to my opponents but equally to my teammates. The coach said, "Your height gives you an advantage, but those braids aren't doing you any good. You should cut them." My answer was "I won't cut them."

When I became a program director at China Central Television, I was fashion-conscious and liked to wear name brands. At the suggestion of a hairstylist who had studied in France, for a time I kept only a little pigtail at the nape of my neck, while the hair up front was combed in a bristling shag. Later upon taking up Buddhism, I became critical of my image in the mirror, and I took to heart what my Grandma had said, "Your hair will have benefits for people, you should let it grow." So I let my hair grow out, until my daughter contracted leukemia and left this world, whereupon I cut it short and used it to cover her head when she was cremated. That evening I had a vision of her spirit cavorting and dancing with a group of white-robed immortals, ascending to the ninth level of heaven. This helped to console me in my grief. Later when I was on Lao Mountain and at other film locations, I missed her so terribly that life held no charm for me. For a time I wanted to do away with myself, but I experienced a series of encounters, each of which came at a critical moment. Many people in China and abroad have read of my account of this.

Grandma passed away shortly before my daughter. One elder

and one child whom I loved above all else both passed away. They had given me a great deal, but they took a great deal from me. Everything that happened in my energy field and consciousness during that period was deposited in my newly growing hair. My hair was short when I went to America, but when I stayed several years in seclusion in the mountains of Malibu, it grew out again. Later I traveled to many places transmitting the wisdom of joyous life and meeting people of all types. Among them I met an ascetic from the Himalayas and several adepts at spiritual practices who each asked for a strand of my hair. They wanted to keep a strand of my hair in a pouch or talisman bag. Some of them even made a place for my hair on their altars. My secretary DaiDai took note of this and gathered strands fallen from my comb, collecting them in a bag. Once she said, "These strands of hair can help people. Let's keep them in reserve." I was struck by the similarity between her words and my Grandma's!

According to knowledge transmitted orally in the Himalayas for thousands of years, hair can be a vehicle which carries many things. My blood carries the genes of wisdom bearers, both Tibetan and Chinese. On top of that, I have found illumination at the edge of life and death. Probably this is why there are people who treat my hair as something precious. As many people know, a chapeaux plaited from the hair of a dakini is an ecstatic vessel that belongs among the world's storehouse of marvels. This is a material thing, yet it enshrines the spiritual attainments of one's progenitors. It is like the Yellow River, the Yangtze or the Yarlung flowing seaward from the source.

There are others who want to grow their hair long for similar reasons. I tell them that their hair can only carry the potency of a "dharma lineage" if their spirits are loving, filled with light and open to what advanced beings have passed down through time. Hair has an inherent connection with lineage—otherwise it will just be a means of self-aggrandizement. This is all the more true in a commercialized milieu where people are impatient for short term advantage.

Long hair is part of my life and I have incorporated a single strand into my shakti paintings within a layer under the painting itself. This imparts greater healing energy to colors and lines in a painting, so it can help one to connect up with universal energies. Long hair has been made into Guanyin figures, and woven into my paintings by an embroidery master of deep spiritual devotion. I have distilled the experiences of the generations before me and my own, to visually express how we sought the Dao, cultivated it and gained realization of it. As a lineage-bearer, I use my life essence as an offering to masters and sages of all eras, while at the same time offering it to all living things.

On the Wings of Phoenix Rising

Phoenix Guanyin

Detail: The image is stitched with hair, not thread.

www.ingramcontent.com/pod-product-compliance
Lightning Source LLC
Chambersburg PA
CBHW060523100426
42743CB00009B/1416